TURIYA
THE GOD STATE

TURIYA: THE GOD STATE

Beyond Kundalini, Kriya Yoga & all Spirituality

- BOOK 5 -

SANTATAGAMANA

Copyright © 2018 by SantataGamana

All rights reserved.

1st Edition, October 2018

ISBN: 978-1728744049

No portion of this book may be reproduced in any form, including photocopying, recording, or any electronic or mechanical methods, without permission from the author except for brief quotes.

Editor: Eric Robins

Design art: Imal8688/Shutterstock.com & Olena1983/Bigstock.com & siro46/Shutterstock.com

Disclaimer for Legal Purposes

The information provided in this book is strictly for reference only and is not in any manner a substitute for medical advice. In the case of any doubt, please contact your healthcare provider. The author assumes no responsibility or liability for any injuries, negative consequences or losses that may result from practicing what is described in this book. Any perceived slights of specific people or organizations are unintentional. All the names referred to in this book are for illustrative purposes only, are the property of their respective owners and not affiliated with this publication in any way.

Read also, by the same author of *Turiya - The God State*:

— KRIYA YOGA EXPOSED

The Truth About Current Kriya Yoga Gurus & Organizations.
Going Beyond Kriya, Contains the Explanation of a Special Technique Never Revealed Before in Kriya Literature.

— THE SECRET POWER OF KRIYA YOGA

Revealing the Fastest Path to Enlightenment.
How Fusing Bhakti & Jnana Yoga into Kriya will Unleash the most Powerful Yoga Ever.

— KUNDALINI EXPOSED

Disclosing the Cosmic Mystery of Kundalini.
The Ultimate Guide to Kundalini Yoga, Kundalini Awakening, Rising, and Reposing on its Hidden Throne.

— THE YOGA OF CONSCIOUSNESS

25 Direct Practices to Enlightenment.
Revealing the Missing Key to Self-Realization. Beyond Kundalini, Kriya Yoga & all Spirituality into Awakening Non-Duality.

— SAMADHI: THE FORGOTTEN EDEN

Unveiling the ancient art of how yogis and mystics had the keys to an unlimited reservoir of wisdom and power.
This book brings the timeless and forgotten wisdom of Samadhi into modern-day practicality.

Available @ Amazon as Kindle & Paperback.

Subscribe and receive the ebook **Uncovering the Real** plus updates and information regarding new books or articles, which will be sent about once a month.

www.RealYoga.info

If you have any doubts or questions regarding this or any of the other books, feel free to contact me at:

Santata@RealYoga.info

Special thanks to Eric Robins, who edited and proofread this book with profound love, kindness, and dedication. Your help has been invaluable.

I have neither Guru nor initiation;
I have no discipline, and no duty to perform.
Understand that I'm the formless sky;
I'm the self-existent Purity.

- Avadhuta Gita

TABLE OF CONTENTS

Semantics	11
Introduction	13
Part I – The Red Pill	**19**
1. The Kernel of Spirituality	21
2. What is Turiya?	25
3. Different Levels of Turiya Integration	35
4. Infusing the Divine Into the Waking State	49
5. The Dreams of Enlightened Beings	57
6. The Ego Paradox	63
Part II – Beyond Known Spirituality	**67**
7. Diving Beneath the Conscious Mind	69
8. Shedding Light Into True Surrender	77
9. Living from Samadhi	89
10. The Dysfunction of Kevala Nirvikalpa Samadhi	95
11. Resisting the Silence	99
12. "You are Already Enlightened!"... or are You?	105

13. Is Enlightenment Having no Thoughts?   111

14. The Myth of Psychological Perfection   117

Part III – Down the Rabbit Hole   **127**

15. The Phantom Enigma   129

16. Only Nothing Survives Forever   139

17. A Simple Trade-Off   145

18. Decoding the God State   151

19. Meet Darkness   155

20. Wake Up Now   159

Glossary   **167**

Semantics

There are books and teachings that talk about *Turiya* and other terms mentioned in this book, but the terminologies used in those teachings might not correlate with their use in this book.

It is requested that you drop your pre-conceived ideas of what Turiya is or isn't. It will be clearer to you what it is by reading this book. Additionally, you can also consult the glossary at the end of the book.

INTRODUCTION

This publication is based on the God State, *Turiya*, which is the highest potential a human can aspire to achieve in the relative manifested world. The God State is a direct consequence of Self-Realization and of the integration of divinity into your life.

Spiritual books rarely talk about the after-effects of Self-Realization and the embodiment of enlightenment in the manifest world.

What makes a good spiritual book is its content; what makes a great spiritual book is the fact that it leads you to yourself, to your true Self.

This book will progressively introduce you to what the God State is, illuminating you with the most in-depth wisdom. This will be followed by a profound and comprehensive explanation and clarification of the intricate processes of surrendering, practice, presence, Parvastha, Self-inquiry, and enlightenment as you've never read before.

As you keep reading, you will encounter special paragraphs and chapters written with the underlying purpose of dismantling the illusory constructs that your ego-mind has created. Some sections, if you give them your full attention, will effortlessly deepen your consciousness into a meditative state, taking you deeper and deeper until you can awaken to pure consciousness, to your own blissful Being. Some phrases are verily a guided meditation that will effortlessly lead you to the absolute silence of Being.

Turiya is an ancient mystery and has been forgotten. It is now time to resurrect it and show you what this God State really is according to the different facets of its manifestation, and also what differentiates it from all other states of being.

The God State is the ultimate expression of a human being in this world; getting rid of the ego is how to start embodying it. By letting go of the density of your habitual mental states, it is time you get to know what your purest divine expression in this world can be. It is time you embody God in this world.

The unseen and immeasurable existence of who we are, once discovered, awakens an instantaneous insight that everything is a speck of dust in comparison to the Ultimate

Reality. But even this speck of dust is worth celebrating once we know our timeless Being. After all, life is a celebration.

The whole of existence is already present within you right this moment, and right now in your life you have all that you need to realize it—regardless of circumstances.

This speck of dust that our relative existence is amasses everything you've ever done, everyone you've ever loved, everyone you've ever known, every human that has ever existed, every enlightened being, every ignorant being, every practitioner, every skeptic, every explorer of consciousness, every scientist, every sage, every fool, every saint, every killer, and every savior. Every act of love toward one another, every sharing of profound life-changing wisdom, every altruistic and genuine smile compose this speck of dust.

This speck of dust, no matter how meaningless it is in the absolute sense, is important to us in our relative existence. Not because of any importance in particular given by the labeling mind—but its apparent existence is supposed to be a celebration of love. Turiya makes that celebration possible!

This book is therefore merely an instrument of remembrance and a guide to help you to awaken from your misleading idea of being a person—a limited, temporary and ego-centered entity. I want to show you that you are God, and no, this is not blasphemy. You will recognize this not through words, but through your own acknowledgment of being inexhaustible bliss itself.

Only by investigating our apparent self and reality will we access the depth of our true Self, in a way often not necessarily understood by the logical mind. What this book talks about can become a trap if used by the intellect—or it can be the confirmation of the perfume that your Heart has been emanating for quite some time.

The teachings in this work are the natural progression of the non-dual yogic teachings in this series. This book is thus not for beginners, but for ardent seekers of the Truth. Having said that, if you have a spark in your Heart for genuine Freedom, then indeed you are not a beginner—you are already well ahead of many, because it is that very desire for God, for the supreme, for realizing your true nature that will take you all the way. And I can confidently confirm that, just by virtue of the fact that you are reading these words, *you do have that spark*. Don't let your ego-mind convince you otherwise.

Living from Turiya is Grace in action, and this book gives a detailed view of how enlightenment manifests differently in each realized human being, for its integration process and subsequent expression are not the same for everyone.

The usually erroneously interpreted "degrees of Enlightenment" will be described as well. There are no degrees of Enlightenment, but there are degrees of the dualistic manifestation of the Truth in our present vehicle of relative expression. This directly corresponds to our body-mind's integration of the light of Awareness, and to its ability to act as a mirror and reflect Self-Realization in this world. This will be elucidated in precise detail.

Amongst countless other subjects, this book will disclose the myths of psychological perfection as well as the reason why the perfect "being" or perfect "Guru" doesn't truly exist. It will be revealed if enlightened Masters still exhibit tendencies, apparent desires, residual habits, and in addition we will explore the pertinent traps concerning such idealized figures.

We have undergone a long journey since *Kriya Yoga Exposed*, the first book of this *Real Yoga* series. We are now approaching its end, and just like in our spiritual path, the abyss of the unknown lies ahead. An encounter with darkness and death—the most terrifying yet important moment in our journey—will ignite the flame of inherent divinity back into the deepest recesses of your Heart. It is my hope that this book enlightens your journey through all abysses, all barriers, and all unconsciously self-created obstacles. I know it will, for you are not alone.

How would your life be if you were struck by the realization that everything you perceive, beyond the ordinary and uninspiring surface, beyond the common faults and labeling that our minds constantly do, is actually an extraordinarily sublime, inseparable and charming treasure that sings in joy in total unison with you? This is truly godly, and yet is inherent to you.

Real enlightenment will annihilate you and subsequently turn you into God. The waters of surrender and the fire of awareness will merge, dissolving the ego into thin air and allowing the one unborn Consciousness, hiding behind "I," to shine through you, as you.

Dive in—with no oxygen tank—it's a one-way ticket to the Unfathomable.

PART I
THE RED PILL

Just because you were born, don't assume that you are truly alive. Being born is what gives you the freedom to actually be alive—and euphorically dance and sing with the whole of creation—if you choose to.

Are you ready to take the red pill?

CHAPTER 1
THE KERNEL OF SPIRITUALITY

Spirituality is becoming more and more mainstream. Having access to deep spiritual truths and practical instructions is as easy as ordering fast food online. Is this a good thing?

In a sense—yes, because you don't have to wash the floors of a Master's temple in the Himalayas for ten years in order to be taught. But in another sense, you may be deceived by increasingly subtle spiritual concepts and fantastical beliefs about what enlightenment and spirituality are or are not, leading you to believe in the myths of psychological perfection.

Additionally, most people use the spiritual path as a means of escaping from their lives in order to avoid facing their traumas and their problems. For this reason, they end up retreating more and more into their egoic minds rather than going deeper into the exploration of consciousness.

Most people no longer use the word "God," and instead are now using non-representational terms such as "Being," "Consciousness," "Awareness," "Infinity," "Absolute," and "Self." Although these expressions make "God" more understandable and relatable in this modern era, they also make it misleading easy to believe that one has grasped the essence of the word "God." At a subtle level, even these non-concrete terms can inhibit the mind from realizing its true nature if it clings to them as concepts rather trying to find what they point toward.

But what is really the final purpose of spirituality?

It certainly is not self-development or aspiring to achieve a perfect personality. That will never happen. Is it wholeness, a union with the whole so that one never feels any sort of lack or desire, which automatically awakes in oneself a deep and permanent sense of happiness, peace, and completeness?

Yes, that's a good start to understanding. Realization of our true nature is the goal, which automatically implies the transcendence of this dualistic and material manifested world and its intrinsic separateness and divisiveness. The realization of being the deathless, unborn and immutable consciousness is the whole purpose of spirituality.

However, one thing must not be forgotten. Although this

realization carries with it the seal of transcendence, it also comes with the subsequent non-intellectual insight that immanence equals transcendence. We transcend this world and realize that there's no difference between it and beyond it.

The coin of Consciousness has two sides: the unmanifested Absolute (*Brahman*), which stays ever the same, ever perfect, and ever fulfilled; and the manifested relative (*Maya*), which never stays the same, and is always evolving and changing. This manifested relative is a journey that never ends, but it often gets neglected in spirituality. In truth, however, the unmanifested Absolute is the same as the manifested relative. They both belong to the coin of Consciousness.

Self-Realization that does not base itself on unity is not real; it is merely a rejection of human existence. We must not deny our humanness—we must embrace it and realize its innate Divinity.

We don't have to die or go anywhere to realize that God is us! We have to achieve this realization while living; we have to find it in our own inner depths and manifest it in our lives. We are going through this ride of self-discovery, getting to know and awakening different facets of our dynamic consciousness. This process brings to the surface long forgotten parts of our once believed identity so that we can realize their falsehood and *involute* back to the kernel of our being—

that which sustains the whole of manifestation—the still ocean of unmanifested consciousness.

We have the honor, the pleasure, and the privilege of being part of the most auspicious journey in the universe, and regardless of whatever obstacles we may face in this road to Freedom, we shall never forget: all of these sacrifices are nothing compared to the bliss of recognizing the ultimate nature of who we are.

We are truly blessed. Tears of joy roar up from our hearts, for we have found the way out of our cage of suffering. The journey of being human has now led us to our birthright—the pure freedom of being God. This is where it all starts—and where it all ends.

CHAPTER 2

WHAT IS TURIYA?

Human beings experience three main states: wakefulness, dreaming and sleeping.

In wakefulness, you experience the world, your memories, goals, likes, dislikes, feelings, thoughts, emotions, sensations, and so on. You have a personality, an identity, and a story. You wake up, live your daily life, and then at night you go to sleep. When you fall asleep, there is a blackout, with some dreams interspersed, and then you wake up again and resume your day. This goes on from the time you were born until the time you die, many decades later. The waking state is the state of ordinary consciousness for the vast majority of beings (99%). Spiritual progress and subsequent realization occur mostly in this state.

Each night, or whenever you fall asleep, you dream. Even if you don't remember any of your dreams in the morning, that doesn't mean you haven't dreamed—it just means you don't remember them.

All minds dream when they disconnect from their physical vehicle. A dream is also very similar to the waking state, in the sense that you experience a world, memories, goals, likes, dislikes, feelings, thoughts, emotions, sensations, and so on (that you totally believe are yours). You have a "dream" personality, a "dream" identity, and a "dream" story. You can even wake up inside of the dream, live your dreamy daily life, and at night (in the dream), you go to "sleep." Although there are some apparent differences, the dream and the waking state are quite similar. Yes, there are inconsistencies in the dream state that you may deem impossible in the waking state, but these are only noticed upon waking up. When you are dreaming, everything seems perfectly fine to you—it is only after waking up that you recognize how impossible and illogical that dream actually was. There can be some spiritual progress in this state, depending on how you approach it. The dreaming state is, therefore, the realm of the subconscious mind.

In addition to these two states, there is also a third state: deep dreamless sleep. This is the so-called "blackout" or "unconscious" state, where there is nothing. The mind has been shut off and the only thing experienced is nothingness—

the absence of experience. There are no objects to be experienced; there is only an empty vacuum of nothingness.

Deep dreamless sleep is the most profound and "out-of-here" repose a typical human being can achieve; it is rejuvenating. This is because the individual consciousness is temporarily deactivated during that state. When you are sleeping, in deep sleep, the ego is in suspended animation, as if it were hibernating. It will then seem to come back and reconstitute itself due to its desire to experience, to live, and to exist as a separate entity. Because there is still life-force in your body, you are obviously not dead, but you are unconscious in a way that resembles death.

From the unenlightened mind's perspective, this state is total darkness and nothingness, but it seems to be the only way that all unrealized living beings can momentarily recoil into the Source, experiencing an unconscious unity with God. It appears to be the opposite of "I am," the opposite of being aware and present. It's an absence—an absence of the totality of the ego and mind. There can be no spiritual progress in this state.

Is there any other state besides these three? Yes, the so-called *superconscious* state of enlightened beings. This is *Sahaja Samadhi*, the natural state. This state is the permanent state of those who realize their true nature. Its main characteristic is the absence of the sense of being a doer; the absence of feeling like a separate entity from the rest of the world (egoless).

What about Turiya then?

There are countless misinterpretations, theories, and conceptualizations about what Turiya is or is not. Most of these teachings are just spiritual mazes that do not help genuine seekers. Turiya may be a difficult subject to explain, but I will clarify it in the simplest possible way while never losing sight of its essential purpose.

The body-energy-mind system of human beings undergoes immense change during the journey "toward" Self-Realization, but even more so after realizing their true nature. This change is perpetuated by the perfume that is emanated from pure awareness, from the substratum, from God Himself.

Turiya can be said to be the outcome of the integration of that perfume into the lives of enlightened beings, thereby transforming them. If enlightenment is the non-dual realization of the Truth, Turiya is the result of the download of that Truth into your body-energy-mind system. This download is special because it updates not only your operating system but also the hardware itself into an entirely new super system.

It is certain that you, as a body-energy-mind system, cannot download the Truth, per se. What is downloaded after Self-Realization is a godly operating system and hardware that will replace your current human operating system and hardware. This update is the ongoing integration of Turiya into your life.

This is the highest state of manifestation that a human being can express, and it possesses all of the godly qualities of peace, love, bliss, wisdom, completeness, and so on. Hence, it is called "The God State." This is Turiya, "The Fourth." It is called "The Fourth" because it is beyond the states of waking, dreaming, and sleeping—it transforms all three into the God State[1].

In this state, the individual mind is reposing in its own source, Sat-Chit-Ananda (Being-Consciousness-Bliss), otherwise known as the Spiritual Heart[2]. Here, a human being is no longer a human being at all—but rather a living

---

[1] It is due to our long habit of considering as real the states of wakefulness, dreaming and sleep, that we call the state of Self-Realization "The Fourth." In fact, there is no fourth state because once the fourth state is, it is the only state, and thus it loses its meaning as the fourth state (all states stand revealed as Turiya itself). However, to facilitate the explanations and communications in this book, I will continue mentioning Turiya and the other three states from the conventional perspective of there being four states.

[2] Refer to Kundalini Exposed, chapter 12 "The Secret Kundalini Throne" and to the Glossary.

incarnation of the Divine. Turiya is truly the highest embodiment of bliss and wisdom that a human can achieve.

The difference (and it is a big one) between deep dreamless sleep and Turiya is that you retain full consciousness in Turiya, while you are unconscious during deep sleep. Therefore, deep sleep with awareness = Turiya.

But, you may ask, if there's nothing during deep sleep, how can there be Turiya during wakefulness?

If enlightenment meant the inability to perceive the world and have the dual experience of dynamic Consciousness, then enlightenment would be limited. From the point of view of the mind, of this world, you can say that wakefulness has its limitations because it's a dualistic state prone to suffering and dissatisfaction. But you could also say that deep sleep has its limitations due to its lack of awareness, its inability to perceive the world and its apparent nothingness/darkness.

How then can non-duality perceive duality?

That's where Turiya comes into play. Turiya is how duality can be perceived without separation—as a wholeness. You perceive the world as you, as Self, without separation, as if deep sleep merged with wakefulness, originating "Wakeful Sleep."

It is being aware and present in absence—the acknowledgment of the light of Awareness in the total darkness of nothingness, and the recognition of Existence in the apparent realm of non-being. It is as if the state of deep sleep were infused with awareness, presence, and light.

This God State is automatically "experienced" every day by everyone in deep sleep, but they just aren't consciously aware of it. It infuses and transforms all states in a realized being, but its integration process happens only after our Kundalini has arrived and is reposing in the Spiritual Heart (Self-Realization).

This state is characterized by an intense and powerful bliss, alongside deep peace and unending wisdom. Some seekers who have had what are usually called "enlightenment experiences" do experience glimpses of the God State to some extent, but then their egoic sense of self comes back and superimposes itself on this blissful substratum of being. During those times, before the seeming return of the ego, they might feel like "How could it ever not be like this? This is so natural and joyful. It has never not been like this...". This is quite right. How can it not be like that? If you've ever had such a glimpse, you should deeply investigate why it is not always like that.

In the relative world, Turiya only manifests in humans

through the "Transcendental-I"[3]. This "I" is not the same as the "I-ego" because it does not suffer and it doesn't perceive everything as separate from itself, but rather experiences life as a continuous and unified presence of Oneness. Turiya is actually the kernel of the "Transcendental-I," the first emanation of the Absolute unmanifested: Pure Bliss (ananda).

Once the physical, energetic, and mental bodies have become capable of sustaining the high degree of bliss and peace that uninterruptedly pour from "within," some level of Turiya has been integrated, and it becomes the natural "active condition" of your body-mind existence. This is the natural state of a human being. Our expression has become totally transparent, fully divine, and according to whatever it is that we are supposed to do in this world, our vehicle will gradually transmute itself into the best possible instrument for that particular dance of life.

---

[3] Refer to *Kundalini Exposed,* chapter 12 "The Secret Kundalini Throne" and to the Glossary.

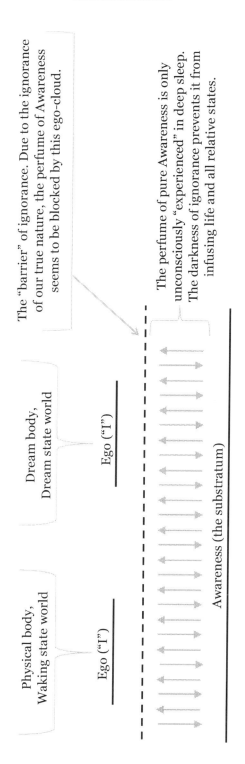

Turiya: The God State

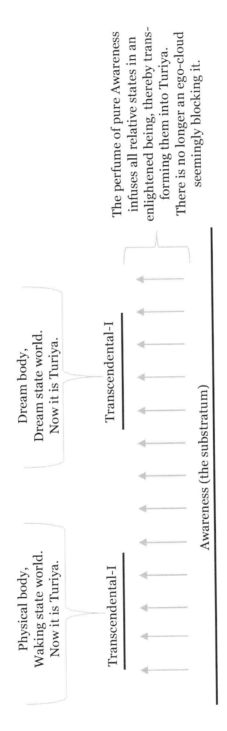

TURIYA IN ENLIGHTENED BEINGS

CHAPTER 3

DIFFERENT LEVELS OF TURIYA INTEGRATION

There is only one Turiya, but there are different levels of it regarding its dual manifestation. For it to grow in depth, your mind, energy and body must already be entirely stabilized and emerged into the God State, which will permeate your life ever more strongly and subsequently turn your vehicle of expression into the perfect embodiment of God. This is not something that is "done," rather it is allowed to naturally happen by being in a state of receptivity and "melting-bliss."

The light of Awareness first infuses the mind, and only afterward does it impregnate the energetic and physical bodies. The process of Turiya integration progressively goes from the subtler to the grosser levels. The whole spectrum of our being must be totally liberated from its usual density and feelings of being a localized entity (including the very act of perception). This progressive integration and assimilation happens in the objective manifest world, and is thus subject to time.

The following are the degrees of integration of Turiya. There is no longer a separate feeling of "I" in any of them, hence in none of these degrees are enlightened beings under the assumption of being doers or of having an ego-self. Keep in mind that although all these degrees are of enlightened beings, there are no degrees of enlightenment[4].

There are degrees of the dualistic manifestation of the Truth in our present vehicle in direct correlation to the body-energy-mind's integration of the light of Awareness, and its ability to act as a mirror and reflect Self-Realization through its expression. These degrees of Turiya integration are usually erroneously interpreted as "degrees of Enlightenment," giving rise to the usual comparisons that seekers make between enlightened Masters.

Level 4 is not truly an "integration" of Turiya, in and of itself, but more like a total absorption of all relativeness into the unmanifested Absolute. I only call it "level" out of simplicity.

---

[4] Refer to *The Yoga of Consciousness*, chapter 8 "Spirituality Can Be the Ego's Playground."

Degrees of integration of Turiya:

(Level 1)

Perceiving duality with a permanent current of joy that grows and expands. The body and the mind are fully active. There are still samskaras and vasanas. Patterns or reactions arising from old habits can still occur, but they don't bring any suffering. There is an intuitive inner knowingness of one's true nature, which is stronger than any previous conviction of being a "man, age 40, born in Barcelona" or a "woman, mother, and lawyer from Massachusetts" for example. This knowingness never fades from now on, and is not based on belief nor thought. There is also the direct insight beyond thought of the unity of everythingness.

The expression "Everything is the Self" is truly understood and known with maximum clarity and certainty. It's not a concept or a supposition; it's pure knowingness. It's as if you were in a dream, fully aware and cognizant of the fact that everything there was only your mind, manifesting in all those forms. The majestic joy of Turiya profoundly affects your relative existence, and it begins to remodel the whole essence of your dual expression. Maya is truly realized to be the Self.

There is an undifferentiated continuum of perception where

despite being able to discern objects, no boundaries are created in relation to their essence. One is like a goldsmith who, rather than seeing all of the different forms of jewelry, sees only gold.

There is a growing unification of the individual life-force with the cosmic life-force; this is the downpouring of the Cosmic Kundalini into our manifested vehicle of expression—Grace infuses our atoms with immaculate divine happiness. The mind has truly been transformed into a pure transcendental mind.

(Level 2)

All of the above, with the addition that duality is perceived with an even stronger joy, love and peace[5]. It is indeed much stronger than level 1 in this regard. The Cosmic Kundalini has integrated to a greater degree into our manifested vehicle of expression. Our atoms are made of Grace itself. The life-force and energetic body have truly been transformed into a pure emanation of being.

The body and the mind may be fully active, but there's a decreasing will to perform activities or to do anything. The

---

[5] This joy, love, and peace are obviously still permanent (just like in level 1). This is akin to increasing the size of a mirror (body-energy-mind) that is reflecting the sun (pure consciousness). The size of the sun doesn't change, but a bigger mirror can reflect more of the sunlight.

enlightened being enjoys and increasingly prefers to sit in silence rather than act. There are still subtle "positive" samskaras and vasanas, subtle habits that the body and mind have accumulated, but these pose no obstruction to the manifested expression of the Truth.

(Level 3)

Perceiving duality as if it were a dream-like world, with a permanent and non-localized universal bliss, love and peace. Physicality in the waking state seems to be made of "dream stuff."

Duality is interconnected as a unified field of experience. Either there is no localized center of attention, in which case the experience goes on impersonally in a non-local way, as if there were no subject at all ("no-I"); or, the center of attention in the body expands its outreach, and seems to be connected to manifestation from that particular point of view (all-encompassing "I")[6].

Just like when you perceive and sense the presence of your hand, and you know that it's connected to you, Oneness may be experienced from the point of view of the body-

---

[6] Although it seems like two different kinds of examples, they are the same. Having no "I" implies that the perceiving mind is unified with the whole; and an all-encompassing "I" implies that there's no "I" as we know it (a separate entity).

mind. E.g., you look at a tree, and you sense and see the tree as yourself—as if you were sensing and looking at your own hand. You know and feel that it's all connected and One (this "center-here yet circumference-everywhere" point of view may also happen in level 2 of Turiya integration, but in that instance, it is not a permanent point of view from the body-mind).

Here's another way of attempting to explain this:

Whenever you finally acquire a new item that you've desired for so long, you feel sort of a connection to it. Let's say you get a new expensive car that you've wanted for so long: you feel great whenever you are in it or think about it, you are overzealous with it, etc.

If we go a bit deeper, we can see that this connection is even stronger with a pet for example. And with a son, daughter, or a loved life partner, it goes even further. The love you feel for that significant other is a profound connection beyond anything physical. If your love for them is powerful enough, you feel connected to them, as if you were only one.

Such experiences of love are glimpses of the love of Oneness. Love is truly the experience of unity. Your "I" which used to feel like a separate entity, is now a "Transcendental-I" which has an expanded outreach encircling everything else, not just the body. This "Transcendental-I" has the whole of creation as its body.

The undifferentiated continuum of perception has dissolved to the maximum possible extent, such that despite still being able to discern objects, no boundaries are created with them in relation to what would usually be called "I" (in this case, in relation to the "Transcendental-I"). The body, which is the grossest expression of a human being, has finally been fully infused and saturated with the light of Awareness, turning perception itself into transparent and reflective wholeness.

"Everything is the Self" is not in one's "state" anymore because one even loses the distinction between "everything" and "Self." There is only the Self. It's more than a profound knowingness, it is as if the five senses collapse without collapsing, encompassing everything but maintaining the lucidity to perform activity and discern between things.

Body and mind are partially active, but it's difficult to perform activities or do anything because the bliss has become too strong to allow engagement with normal daily living. Most of the time, the enlightened being prefers to sit in silence rather than act, although they can speak, interact and move if they wish. There are still subtle sattvic (pure) conditionings which would be detrimental to erode because they fit this particular body-mind and its potential destiny of expressing the Truth in this world.

(Level 4)

Talking about this doesn't do justice to its reality. It's like attempting to convey silence through words. Nonetheless, an attempt to convey this level will be made:

Non-perceiving duality, fully emerged and absorbed by rapture and peace. Either the body lies like a corpse and there is an "inability" to speak, interact, move or think; or if any action is performed, it is akin to a toddler drinking milk while asleep, and without being aware of anything (no body-awareness)[7]. There is non-local and non-temporal awareness. No samskaras, no vasanas. It's as if you were dead, but you are alive. No "Transcendental-I," no anything. All levels of both the subtle vestiges of individuality and of extreme transcendence have been totally annihilated.

There can be said to be a last vasana which consists of an extremely subtle level of pseudo-individuality. This remains in potentiality, so that it is possible to interact and perceive the world through the "Transcendental-I" if this human being fluctuates between level 4 and level 3. With that being

---

[7] To an external observer though, that toddler will appear to be acting (drinking).

said, if a being remains for too long in full-blown Turiya, then this extremely subtle vasana may revert from potentiality back to nothingness. Such a happening is extremely rare though.

There is no "Everything is the Self" or "There is only Self," because everything in relativity collapses. There is no everything or even the "Self." Those were mere concepts created by our limited minds to help our understanding and integration of the Truth into our temporary human existence.

Understand that this degree of Turiya is not similar to Kevala Nirvikalpa Samadhi (temporary formless absorption where the ego returns afterward). In Turiya, a Self-Realized being is at all times absorbed in the Self. It doesn't matter whether they are sleeping, moving, sitting, lying like a corpse, talking, laughing, crying, etc. That being IS the Absolute.

However, what is being mentioned here is related to the state of the body-mind in this manifested world. The Absolute, which is an enlightened being's true Self, is not subject to states; on the contrary, the relative counterpart consisting of a mental, energetic and physical vehicle is. Hence this is merely a way of demonstrating the understanding of the dualistic expression of such a being.

The strongest embodiment of Turiya while being active and

engaging in the world is level 3, although some sages and saints' body-mind have interchanged between levels 3 and 4 throughout their lives. The highest manifestation of life as a human being is thus not level 4, and it is easy to realize why—in such "state," the pure mind remains entirely absorbed in its source, unwaveringly, and no spark of relative consciousness "comes out." Only in levels 1, 2 and 3 does consciousness still seem to appear as a unified manifestation to the extroverted outlook of the mind.

Although the example of a movie theater is not perfect, it may help to clarify the understanding:

State	**Movie playing**	**Lights**
Waking State	Yes	Off
Dream State	Yes	Off
Deep Sleep	No	Off
Turiya	Yes	On
Turiyatita (level 4)		On, max. brightness

Whenever the lights are off, it's a clear sign of ignorance. Whenever the lights are on, it's a clear sign of realization. The deeper Turiya infuses your life, the stronger the light. With mild light, you can still slightly see the movie, but you know it's a play of consciousness, an illusion, something temporary; with the lights at maximum brightness, you won't see any movie—you only see light. The dichotomy of there being a movie or no movie has been transcended.

Rare beings whose realization propelled them to level 4 may have to naturally integrate Turiya back to level 3. This is, therefore, not a downgrade, but an improvement in their ability to operate in the world and naturally help it expand and evolve into a deeper collective consciousness. The most common level of expression for enlightened Gurus and Masters is level 1 and 2. Few are at level 3, and most of these are not publicly known nor are they available to the masses.

Many of those in level 1 and 2 get too active with teaching right after realizing their true nature (level 1) and the natural integration of Turiya (level 2 and 3) never "occurs." Perhaps their purpose in this world is such that they have to stay with their current degree of embodiment of the Truth until late in their lives or even until death.

Once you reach level 3 there is no way of going back to levels 1 and 2. Life and the world will just seem too meaningless and illusory for you to have any will in actively participating in them. The bliss is too intense in level 3 to live an active life. In level 1 you can do it perfectly, but after level 2 it gets "harder."

Most enlightened beings, at the time of their physical death, naturally "move" into level 4 and dissolve their transcendental existence forever. A rare exception is those who remain with a subtle embodiment in subtler realms of relative existence, for a particular universal purpose, until they too naturally "move" on to level 4.

Level 4 at its splendor could also be called *Turiyatita*, "Beyond the Fourth." This is because in Turiyatita, which is synonymous with the Absolute point of view, there is no world, no body, no life, no humans, no universes, no mind, no thoughts, no anything, no nothing, no not-nothing, no waking state, no dreaming state, no deep sleep, and no degrees of Turiya integration. Turiya is thus Turiyatita because in the highest degree of its integration, there is no integration and no perception nor non-perception. It is beyond presence and absence because from its point of view, everything and nothing collapse. This means that we could label level 1, 2, 3 and 4 of Turiya integration as Turiya, but we could only label Turiyatita as level 4, because the apparent allowance for the overlap of the manifested creation no longer exists nor has it ever existed in such an absolute perspective.[8]

---

[8] Such perspective, although absolutely true, is beyond the scope of *all* books because there are no books, no teachings, no students, no seekers, and no enlightened beings from it; hence there would be nothing to say. It's not even correct to call it a "perspective." Refer to *Beyond Shiva* or *Ashtavakra Gita* for a deep non-linear read on this subject.

Sahaja Samadhi and Turiya

Let's not confuse Turiya with Sahaja Samadhi. Sahaja Samadhi is the permanent realization of our natural state and of our true Self, and all the depths of integration of Turiya are sustained in Sahaja Samadhi (level 1 through 4), which is the beyond-the-mind Self-Awareness of our true nature.

Sahaja Samadhi = permanent realization of our true nature; the end of the ego.

There can be Sahaja Samadhi with different degrees of embodiment of the Truth. Don't let this statement deceive you though; Self-Realization is still rare! It may be rare, but you are well on your way to finding this treasure, which is what everyone is searching for, even if they don't know it yet.

CHAPTER 4

INFUSING THE DIVINE INTO THE WAKING STATE

The majority of human beings live their lives somewhere between the waking state and the dreaming state. Every time they are lost in thought, daydreaming, etc., their physical surroundings get dimmed and they can even become totally oblivious to their environment. This condition is a mix between wakefulness and the dream state, and it is also the dimension of creativity, imagination, etc. Thus few humans are ever truly lucid, present or really conscious.

In the waking state, no matter how deep we go into our own consciousness, if we wish to remain active and engaged in the world, we (as body-minds) have to retain an "I." Hopefully by now you have come to understand that the "I" we want is not the common "I," known as ego, but rather the "Transcendental-I."

The "Transcendental-I" retains an extremely subtle impersonal individuality that poses no obstacle whatsoever, but merely allows the body-mind to stay alive and experience this world (in spite of this experiencing being characterized by unity rather than by diversity as is prevalent in the human ego-mind).

When fully "integrated" and "stabilized" into our own waking consciousness[9], the state of Turiya is reflected in our intellect, which becomes *sattvic* (pure) and allows us to maintain a subtle connection to our human expression.

In Self-Realization, we have realized the root of who we are. We have dived deep into the Unmanifested and yet, from the relative position of our dual existence as ever-evolving body-minds, we continue our relationship with the manifested. Life in this world proceeds, through the five gross senses, but the "Transcendental-I" that lives "in" this body is as if it were Life itself living itself effortlessly, rather than an individual thought called "I." The mind, the senses, and all of our natural human functions are never abandoned, unless we (as body-minds) want to lie in death-like yet conscious blissful Samadhi until the body dies.

---

[9] This is from the mind's perspective, because it is neither truly integrated nor stabilized; rather the old and residual mental tendencies and impressions, psychological imprints, and subtle habits progressively fade out.

Our beingness is anchored in the Self, in subjectivity, but the flow of divine intelligence, pure love and bliss have yet to fully express themselves through this human vehicle. This is something that nothing can prepare us for, regardless of how much purification and preparation our system has gone through before Self-Realization.

This God State is not at all prevalent in the majority of today's known "gurus" or "masters" because most of them only have an intellectual understanding of the Truth; or, because despite having had powerful insights, it still wasn't *the ultimate Insight.* In some cases, it might be that their Self-Realization is still at a level which has yet to translate into palpable energy, presence and body-mind state (manifestation-wise speaking) in comparison to the ancient yogis, sages and saints.

This brings up a big "problem." Once the ultimate Insight of our true nature spontaneously "occurs," we as body-minds lose any interest whatsoever in the embodiment of the Divine.

First, because we know that everything is Divine. Second, because there is no more seeking or will to search because nothing lacks. It is an arrival without ever having left. Third, because we know we are bodiless, there's no reason, strength or will to "update" the body-mind so that it can be a purer expression of God. There's even no "I" that could ever want or need to be a "purer expression of God." There's no feeling of being the doer.

So how can we "solve" this? It is easy. We merely have to "do" what ancient yogis, saints, and sages have done. What is that?

Nothing.

Nothing, but being silent.

That is all. For those who have realized their true nature, sitting in silence (rather than attempting to start giving workshops, retreats, initiations, etc.) is the best thing they can "do."

This will hasten the integration and stabilization of Self-Realization into the body-energy-mind more than anything else. No, no more practice is necessary. This doesn't mean that one can't or shouldn't do any activity, and it doesn't mean one can't or shouldn't teach or speak. It merely means that one should preferably keep quiet and stay in silence. This is how the true God State of pure infinite bliss will naturally become more and more present in the human body-mind system. It's the melting of our grosser vehicles of expression into their eternal source; the soaking of the *knowingness* of our true nature into itself.

The body, due to its grosser vibration, typically takes longer to be impregnated with the perfume of realization; there are still vestiges not yet bathed by the light of Self-Realization. Eventually, Turiya will engulf the body and our perceived sensations in relation to it as well.

For over 20 years after his realization, Ramana Maharshi sat in caves in near silence. His realization was *the same* all throughout this time, from the moment he realized his deathless nature at age 16 until he dropped his body at age 70. But his dual expression changed. He went from being entirely absorbed in level 4 Turiya like a corpse, where ants were literally eating his flesh while he was utterly oblivious to the world, to level 3, which enabled him to talk, write and share his supremely divine teachings with the world. His case is not an ideal example because Self-Realization sky-rocketed his consciousness instantly to level 4 of Turiya. Although this can happen, it is extremely rare. Usually it starts at level 1 and progressively goes higher. In Maharshi's case, the integration of Turiya in his system led him from level 4 to level 3, which is the perfect state from which one can teach the most profound spiritual teachings to the world. From a relative perspective, this was not a downgrade but was actually an improvement in his ability to perform and instill knowledge in and into the world. We have his written teachings available today thanks to this.

Other genuine Masters had their relative consciousness go through slightly different types of integrations and assimilations, but the principle behind the depth of Turiya is the same. This means that even though two different beings might be Self-realized, their expression in this world might be entirely different, for they may have different purposes.

Turiya is usually understood as a "brush-off" of the waking state, which views the world as non-important. But this is not correct. Turiya in the waking state is not a negation of life or of our fellow human beings, but just the opposite! It is a total embrace of our humanity and of every living being in the universe. We enter into a harmonious dance with the totality of creation, awakening in ourselves the absolute state of God, embodying the pure qualities and presence of the universal consciousness of God. This is the true meaning of the word Avatar. It is the descent of the Universal Consciousness (Cosmic Kundalini, "I Am" or Shakti) into our relative consciousness, which expands and dissolves the totality of physical boundaries of a locale and individual body-awareness.

The problem with calling Turiya "The Fourth State," the state of transcendence, while referring to the waking, dreaming and sleep states as "ordinary human-consciousness states," is that this brings a negative connotation to these states, especially to the waking state from where our world is perceived. Notwithstanding, realization can only occur within the waking state (very rarely from the dream state), hence making this state the most important one to realize our true nature! Clearly, deep sleep is not a state apt for spiritual practice (the abilities to witness, reflect, concentrate, meditate, etc., have been suspended), and the dream state is very volatile, with the most progress made there being related to the assimilation and dissolution of subconscious trauma.

For a realized being, the waking state is not a prison, nor does it clash with Turiya. Seekers of the Truth should be thankful for the waking state rather than trying to avoid or escape from it by going into deep Samadhis, alternative states of mind, or absorptions that lead nowhere. It is important to notice that the waking state is actually the portal to realization; it is the only state where spiritual practice can be done![10]

Moreover, after Self-Realization, the waking state does not

---

[10] If the waking state consciousness is brought upon the dreaming state, then this state can too be useful for spiritual practice, being much more powerful and magical than the waking state—but also more elusive, unstable and trapping. Unlike in the opaqueness of the waking state, in the volatility of the dream state, consciousness has contact with a more expansive portion of its limitless potentiality. This is an entirely different topic though, and would require a completely new volume to be addressed.

evaporate into nothingness. Our "I" is gone, but as has been mentioned, the "Transcendental-I" is here, and it will stay until the end of the body.[11] This makes the waking state extremely important.

The God State is God *consciously* walking on Earth as a human being. This happens in wakefulness. Humans who embody this pure state ultimately go beyond the need of going beyond. They are God, knowing that they are God with every cell of their being.

---

[11] Obviously, this is merely from the mind's point of view, from an outside observer, rather than from the Absolute point of view, in which the world doesn't remain because it never appeared in the first place

CHAPTER 5

THE DREAMS OF ENLIGHTENED BEINGS

We all know how important deep sleep is in our lives when it comes to rejuvenating pranic and mental energy. But just like deep sleep, dreaming is also a fundamental process, allowing a human being's optimal functioning in this world.

Dreaming occurs in order to help us process, reorganize and heal the subconscious mind. It can be very healing because we experience a new dream lifetime there that helps us to solve and/or process whatever internal issues we're having at the moment in our lives. Without dreaming and deep dreamless sleep, the human mind and body would become psychologically and physiologically erratic, which would bring serious mental disorders, possibly culminating even in death.

Do enlightened beings dream then?

The answer to this question comes in different degrees.

First of all, the enlightened being is not the body-mind, but is rather the formless consciousness that is the source of everything. Having had such Self-recognition implies that the enlightened being in question does not identify with their body-mind anymore; hence no dreaming occurs. Pure Consciousness doesn't dream. This is akin to a screen that is self-aware; that screen neither sleeps nor dreams, it is ever wide-awake.

However, when considering the body-mind of enlightened beings, their connection with the dream state always depends on their integration of Turiya.

If the God State has been fully integrated (level 4), the enlightened being will not dream because there is no need for the subconscious mind to process or solve any issues related to that being's life. There's not even a mind. The whole period where the enlightened being's body sleeps is merely a continuity of the natural empty Self-Awareness of Being, without any apparent superimposition whatsoever. The states of waking and sleeping are what an observer's mind would deduct that is happening to that being, when in fact, from that enlightened being's perspective, all there is, is the Self.

If Turiya has been partially integrated, then the enlightened being will dream, but there will be fewer dreams. Additionally, the dreams will not be chaotic or contain anything related to traumas/desires/samskaras/vasanas and so on, but there may be slight resemblances, like the smoke that is still in the sky even after the fire has been extinguished, or the echo of a scream still reverberating in the mountains.

Deeply rooted subtle habits are hard to eliminate from the body-mind, but they will slowly be washed away as Turiya starts naturally and effortlessly becoming more and more integrated into the conscious mind. Occasionally, they can be blasted away by Self-Realization, but more often than not this a gradual process that occurs in the relative realm of consciousness.

Dreams may also be exclusively related to the experience of living, of perceiving and of duality, without any emotional content or attachment. Alternatively, they may occur so that the information that the mind processed throughout the day gets assimilated and consolidated into the intellect, but without posing any issues whatsoever. Dreaming will be like mixing olive oil with pure crystal water; the oil just doesn't color the water—it doesn't color awareness.

Many times these dreams will be an extension of the waking state, in which Turiya emanates from the dream character (which is also a manifestation of the "Transcendental-I") toward the dream world and toward other dream characters, exactly as occurs in the waking state. The waking state body (which is a dream) of the enlightened being also emanates bliss, love, peace, and wisdom towards the waking state world (which is a dream) and toward other people (who are characters within the dream of the waking state). This mostly happens in level 3 of Turiya integration.

These degrees are not black and white; rather they have varying shades of black, grey and white, and depend on each being.

Dreams are just like the waking state; if the waking state appears to superimpose itself as a movie on the empty screen of consciousness, the same happens with dreams. They are co-dependent, and only by erasing the totality of the waking state and the waking world do the dreaming state and dream worlds disappear too.

Understand that even though one could say that the dream characters in the dream state are being dreamed by you (or your individual consciousness) while the dream characters in the waking state are being dreamed by God (or the universal consciousness), such an assertion would be made by the ego, because only the ego can feel itself as being separate from God. It is either you dreaming them all, as God, or God dreaming them all, as you. There's no distinction unless you put on the ego's lens of perception. Furthermore, since the dreams occur within the realm of the subconscious, they can sometimes merge with both the collective consciousness or collective unconscious of humankind, or even of different types of beings.

In all these cases though, enlightened beings never slip from their natural and effortless Self-repose in and as pure awareness itself.

CHAPTER 6

THE EGO PARADOX

Nature and the universe are intelligent—there's no denying that. This universal intelligence is devoid of a sense of self, and operates unselfconsciously, permeating all forms, although it is overlapped by the arising sense of "I" in some animals and humans.

In most animals, that sense of "I" is subconscious, meaning there's only a subliminal sense of a self which is unaware of itself, and that responds and interacts instinctively with the world through sensory input. It is aware non-conceptually of "this is me as this body" and "this is the outside environment," along with a sense of being alive and also an instinctive fear of death.

On planet Earth, discernment concerning the sense of self and the ability to self-observe occurs mostly in humans and in some advanced animals such as dolphins. This observation occurs initially by way of mental reflection and being the subject of the thinking process, which requires intelligence and a developed ego. However, upon passing through a certain threshold of lucidity, this advanced mind starts to become aware of its own subjectivity, which is one of the keys in spiritual practice.

To be able to achieve the process of Self-awareness, the bodily vehicle needs to be highly developed. The earlier cellphones lacked the necessary hardware to be able to play videos or take photographs, but today's smartphones can easily do so due to much more powerful hardware. In the same way, most animals cannot have a conscious experience of self-awareness or even self-reflection because they lack the hardware to do so. Their brain and nervous system are underdeveloped. Without such hardware, the software to run advanced programs will never be created.

It is interesting to note that only after the "I-ego" has become sufficiently advanced (which, as mentioned, requires powerful hardware), can it become aware of its own "I-ness." A tree is intelligent, but not in the same way as human beings. It has no "I" and no ego. It can't be self-aware, but it also has no need to do so as trees and nature work more as a matrix of conscious energy rather than as individual "beings," although some do possess distinctive "traits."

The ego, which is essential for the survival and continuity of the human species, is also necessary so that human beings can go through the process and journey of discovering their own essence, eventually overcoming the ego itself. It is the ego that has this ignorance and suffering "problem" that needs to be transcended. If there is no thinking and no ego, then there's no need to realize non-duality either. Non-duality is ever realized, and it is human consciousness that believes itself to be ignorant and then creates the need to transcend the self-created ignorance, subsequently realizing that there was never any ignorance and no need to transcend it whatsoever.

This is the paradox of humanity and its ego. The vehicle of individuality (ego) is required to become self-conscious of not being the ego, through awareness of its own subjectivity and eternity. It is only after tasting birth and death that we can discover the timeless.

While suffering exists, the potentiality of enlightenment also exists—in fact it is suffering's opposite, located on the other side of the spectrum. If we have gone deep in our journey toward Freedom, we'll realize sooner or later that even enlightenment is ultimately fake. Enlightenment exists only in duality by contrasting it with ignorance. In the same way, the Absolute exists only in contrast to relativeness.

Even in the natural state (Sahaja Samadhi), *from the relative point of view,* there is still the apparent superimposition of the waking and dream states onto pure consciousness. With time, as Turiya gets more and more integrated into our relative existence (level 1 through 3), this contrast reduces gradually until it collapses altogether.

The realization of who we truly are means we have actually been liberated from both enlightenment and ignorance!

PART II
BEYOND KNOWN SPIRITUALITY

To keep living the ignorance of separation is not only insanity but an embracing of claustrophobia.

CHAPTER 7

Diving Beneath the Conscious Mind

The need to create meaning in the experience of life is one of the elemental drives of human nature, and it starts from the time one is very young, continuing all the way until death. All meaning is created by the ego-mind, which unendingly attempts to make sense of what's happening.

All contents that appear in consciousness have to be interpreted and attributed a meaning that makes sense to the ego's self-created concept of itself. If something is in conflict with the ego's story, the ego will either deem it irrelevant and ignore it, allowing it to barely reach the conscious mind, or will interpret it in a way that fits the ego's identity, composing a logical story (from the ego's perspective) so that the ego's reign remains unaffected.

All of the things that the ego doesn't want to accept and

integrate into its narrative (because they would destroy its foundations), or that the ego ignores due to pain, fear of suffering, or just because it's not coherent with its identity, are stored in the subconscious mind. The subconscious mind thus possesses tremendous creative, intelligent and intuitive powers (as can be directly experienced in meditation), as well as a great deal of trauma, suffering, and illogical ways of thinking. While the conscious mind is a narrow field of localized and focused awareness, the subconscious mind is a broader field of "vaguely" localized awareness.

The subconscious mind is scattered throughout the body's nervous system (nadis, chakras) and brain, and also extends beyond the physical body into the energetic field. This energetic field carries within it the seeds that we have previously planted, and manifests itself in different ways every time we dream, for example.

Whenever we do spiritual practice, we are purifying both the conscious and the subconscious mind by increasing the power of our life-force, discernment, wisdom, concentration, mindfulness, awareness and lucidity. By bringing the subconscious contents up to the conscious mind, they can be seen with the eyes of wisdom and realized as not-self. The recognition that they belong to a temporary identity created by a false "I" diminishes the power they have over us by shrinking their mass (our attachment to them), and thus reducing the effect of their gravity (the power they have over us), until they disappear entirely.

With *Kriya Pranayama*, for example, we place so much emphasis on the Third-Eye (Ajna Chakra, the seat of the conscious mind) because we want to bring all the subconscious debris (which are spread-out via prana through the whole body-mind system) into the conscious mind (Ajna Chakra).

When it is said in Kriya Yoga literature that Kriya Pranayama brings *samskaras* up to the Third-Eye where they are destroyed, what that means is the following:

Samskaras is a word that denotes unconscious tendencies, subtle habits and desires, psychological imprints, mental impressions or deep buried emotional traumas. The *Third-Eye* is the focal point related to the Ajna Chakra, which is the seat of the conscious mind. By practicing a technique like Kriya Pranayama, you are stilling your mind both by slowing the breathing process through deep calm breathing, and by having your attention focused rather than being scattered all over the place as it usually is.

This whole process will help you get into a deeper, more peaceful state of consciousness, thereby expanding your conscious mind and connecting it more and more with what was once "unconscious" in you. In these deeper states, those samskaras that are usually lying below your conscious mind are "brought up" to it. By witnessing those mind-contents arising in the space of your awareness (Post-Kriya Awareness, Parvastha), you can see them with much wisdom, remaining calm, tranquil, and with equanimity, and by virtue of this fresh sense of heightened awareness, you can realize that those memories, traumas, emotions, imprints, desires etc. are "not-I" and "not mine."

This whole process creates dispassion/non-attachment in you with respect to the fake "I," its personality, and all of its stories, purifying your consciousness so that it can become ripe for the Self-recognition of its pure stainless nature. That's the real meaning of these ancient yogic terms which are not truly understood by most aspirants these days.

The "Third-Eye" is much more than an "ethereal vortex spinning inside the skull." The point is that people need to get over such concepts if they want to go deeper into themselves toward true spirituality. For example, the concept of "Awakening/opening the Third-Eye" is a figure of speech. What happens in these cases is that the conscious mind expands beyond its usual "waking state limits" into the subconscious mind, enabling it to access a broader range of the subtle manifestations that were previously concealed by the five senses. This allows one to consciously enter into states beyond wakefulness, which are usually confined to trance states, dreaming, hypnosis, etc. Some examples of this include having access to the collective unconscious, seeing subtle symbolic representations with the mind's eye superimposed on the waking state's physical vision, truly seeing what is being visualized or imagined, and so on.

If you do spiritual practice, and by awakening the latent cosmic life-force within you (Kundalini), you will eventually bring all of the unconscious parts of your illusory identity to the surface. As the Kundalini goes higher and higher in your nervous system, your conscious mind starts permeating all of its previously non-conscious parts[12], eventually culminating in the cosmic experience of being the whole of creation. This is akin to a movie character realizing that she is the whole movie, rather than just an individual character.

Many traditions or spiritual organizations consider this to be the final emancipation, the goal of all spirituality. It is

---

[12] When it is written that all the unconscious parts are brought to the conscious mind, this is meant in relation to enlightenment. It does not imply that realizing your true nature will give you access to and control over your digestion process, immune system or metabolic rate. It can, but it probably won't. For these processes to be brought up to the conscious mind, they do require different yogic practices. This explanation should therefore not be taken out of context.

understandable why—you perceive the world as a unity, always filled with bliss and peace. But unless this is a consequence of realization, in which the Kundalini dissolves into the Spiritual Heart, it will only be an experience. This means that such a cosmic experience will pass, and that the "I-ego" will then come back to its normal level of functioning afterward. The only way to stop the re-emergence of the "I-ego" is through enlightenment and subsequent Turiya integration.

Enlightenment is analogous to a movie character realizing that she is the screen where every movie, every character's life, and everything appears and disappears. Turiya integration is the subsequent progressive integration of this recognition into the movie and the character's life itself. It's as if the "I-ego" was swallowed by the Spiritual Heart and then brought back to the surface as the "Transcendental-I."

Once the mind "arrives" in the Spiritual Heart, if it reemerges, that is the "Transcendental-I." This is akin to one of the first 3 levels of Turiya integration.

If the mind entirely and permanently abides in the Spiritual Heart, this is akin to level 4 of Turiya integration, where there isn't even any "Transcendental-I."

If the mind is not even one bit in the Spiritual Heart, then that human being is not enlightened. The bliss of all cosmic Samadhis are no match for the bliss of the Self in the Heart. The former is like the moonlight, while the latter is like a perpetual supernova of bliss.

CHAPTER 8
SHEDDING LIGHT INTO TRUE SURRENDER

Surrender is one of the essential aspects of the spiritual path. True surrendering does not involve performing rituals, devotional worship, or anything of a similar nature—it is much deeper than that. It is the unbroken "act" of letting go toward your own Self.

However, surrender seems to be continuously misinterpreted, misapplied or even distorted. Based on this, I have decided to go much deeper than ever before into its practical explanation to make everything as clear as possible. Surrender is fundamental to our journey and to Self-Realization, and it's intimately connected with "just Being," being aware of awareness, and *Parvastha*.

To clarify, you are present whenever you are aware of being aware; whenever you are *present in the now* rather than *absent* (like when you are lost in thought). Whenever you abide in the background of all experience—the subject to all that is experienced—rather than identifying with the objective experience or with the contents of the mind, then you are present. It is staying as the *knower* (consciousness), rather than as the *known* (objects of consciousness including our chaotic mind-stream or even our identity). Being present and self-aware is also the same state that a practitioner experiences in the after-practice absorption state (Parvastha). This is synonymous with the state of abiding in your own empty awareness after a successful meditation or yogic practice.

Surrendering without enough presence and Self-awareness is not true surrender, and will not get you far. The "I-ego" cannot truly surrender itself; hence you need a keen awareness of the presence of Being to be able to truly surrender. By being aware of presence, we are already surrendering the ego, because we are consciously preventing any movement of the mind from happening.

In our daily lives, our mind is continuously moving from this to that and from here to there. Even in spiritual practice, we are moving the mind from this chakra to that chakra, from this breath to that breath, from this visualization to that visualization, and so on. The total stoppage of all mental movements only happens once the mind abides in its source— empty awareness being aware of its own presence or existence. This is the first step. It is from this state of now-ness/Self-awareness recognition that everything truly starts going deeper.

Nonetheless, you have to prevent yourself from turning abidance-in-presence into the alluring trap of blissful dullness. This means that although you are in a state of bliss, you are only partially aware of being present. Your lucidity is not as sharp as it needs to be. This is not true bliss, but merely an initial glimpse of it.

The next step in surrendering is surrendering our own presence of Being to the presence of Being, not only during spiritual practice, but throughout all activities as well.

What does this mean? Presence is impersonal; it doesn't carry with it the flavor of an identity. The challenge arises when the ego-mind attempts to pocket the presence of Being into its own conditioning and labeling process. It can never really do it, but this can create a fog between your consciousness and its ability to melt into the presence of Being.

Presence is like space: it's everywhere and it has no boundaries. What the ego-mind tries to do is to create an artificial and illusory boundary around a certain "place" in place-less space, as if you were putting fences in an empty field and calling that particular space "My property." Is that really your property, or did you just attempt to limit boundless space into a particular terrain that you now proclaim to possess? The ego tries to do the same with boundless presence, preventing the true surrendering of our individual consciousness into the impersonal universal Consciousness.

You mustn't conclude that you have known your true nature or that "This is the Self," or even that you are correctly practicing objectless meditation if you catch yourself labeling or narrating what's happening. It is too easy for the ego-mind to attempt to categorize this state into "I am present," "I am in presence," "I am abiding in presence," "I am aware of being aware," "I am surrendering," or "This is Parvastha" and create a somewhat spiritual identity from it. Don't attempt to label it.

Surrendering is a delicate process that is hard to convey but easy to understand for those who genuinely practice. You must stay hyper-lucid with full stable attention, yet at the same time you must gently let go, surrendering to the depths of God. It is not merely an act of general relaxation or of "dropping the weight." It must be directed with intention at our own Self, at the essence of our own I-ness.

The balancing of subtle intention, surrendering and lucidity can be difficult to juggle, and it eludes the ability of our conscious mind. That's why through spiritual practice, in the surrendering of simply Being, we naturally merge our conscious mind with our subconscious mind, empowering our natural ability to "perform" the process of surrendering. Intentions from the conscious mind flood into the subconscious mind with exceptional potency, plus this transition greatly trims/shrinks our sense of personal identity, increasing the ability to surrender even more *as long as we stay fully aware*.

The next step is consciously letting go of the need to consciously abide in presence, all while remaining effortlessly present and aware of Being. This is because abidance in presence can become subtle suffering, considering that when we are abiding, we are maintaining a thin line of effort, will, and movement. We are not truly effortlessly at rest yet.

This level of surrendering is achieved with the realization of a constant inner and natural knowingness of Being without the need to consciously be. This effortless Being is automatically "activated" with genuine and continuous practice and surrender[13]. It's like a "click" that suddenly occurs. You suddenly become aware of the fact that you are effortlessly Being.

---

[13] This transition is very well detailed in *The Yoga of Consciousness* chapter 20 - "You Have What It Takes."

This is where many spiritual teachings end. Effortlessly Being is such a pure and deep surrender that it is no wonder why most seekers stay there. In that state, however, you experience yourself more as one who is reposing in effortless Beingness, rather than being Beingness itself. The distinction is that, in the former, there is still one abiding in something greater.

The next step is being absorbed by presence. This absorption is a powerful Samadhi, and it can lead to Nirvikalpa Samadhi where prana stops completely. There is a very fine line that separates both. This is not what we want, because if it happens, the false "I" will not be destroyed. How do you prevent this from happening? It's really inexplicable. You (as presence) "maintain" an awareness of yourself, collapsing all causality and space-time into yourself. This is neither done through effort nor attention. It is a relinquishing of all unconscious friction, the bottom 1% of the subconscious mind. It's difficult to convey via words, but at that precise moment, "you[14]" will know what to "do."

If Nirvikalpa Samadhi happens, that is still an extremely subtle maintaining of identity because it is an expression of freedom from our limited self and mind. Since it has no

---

[14] Not truly "you," but more like the "deeper you;" your purest version so to speak.

permanent continuity and therefore the identity returns, the ego-mind will annex that "experience" as part of its identity and false sense of being.

The processes of both Self-Inquiry (or abiding in Presence/Parvastha/Background of Consciousness), and Surrender go hand in hand. They are actually different ways of reaching the same destination. If we combine them, we'll end up with a potent recipe for Self-Realization. The different levels of depth of this recipe can easily be overlooked. The reason they are usually not mentioned or talked about by anyone, is mostly due to either an inability to differentiate between them or due to superficial direct experience.

First level

The mind is still and just needs to let go for a fraction of a second in order to allow the recognition of the sense of being to arise. This sense of being is "I am," which is presence or awareness of the background of Consciousness. The mind merely needs to become aware of its source—the subject—empty awareness. In some spiritual circles, satsangs or teachings, this is equated with enlightenment, which is an utter absurdity. We can call it the awakening of being aware of a deeper level of being, which was previously colored by over-identification with "doing" and with the mental contents that we seem to love and worship so much.

Second level

After the recognition of blissful empty consciousness, we have to abide there and we have to remember to abide in presence, to constantly be aware of being aware. This is not an effort-free state, but also not a super effortful state. There's a fine line that separates both, and only genuine practitioners can find their own inner balance that makes them steadily abide and melt in that very emptiness. Abiding in presence, as aforementioned, is already the beginning of profound surrender.

Third level

Both the second and the third level can be intermixed since this process is not a straight line. As we consciously abide in presence more and more, just Being, we are also starting to surrender more and more, acquiring a taste of the true effortlessness of being by letting go of the need to be aware of being aware, but still being aware. We still feel as if we were effortlessly resting in awareness, rather than being just pure awareness.

Fourth level

We are absorbed and become Presence or the Witness itself—the observing awareness that is free of all characteristics.

Yet we still have a subtle feeling of "I-ness." It's as if we were the background Witness of everything, but there's still the duality of the background and the foreground.

Final level

At this point, it is easy to sink into total absorption (Samadhi), but then it will only be a temporary experience. We must hold onto the residues of subtle "I-ness" up until the very end, until we reach 100% surrender and pure non-dual Self-Awareness. Then the "I" will be extinguished entirely. There will no longer be a subject of absorption or surrendering, but only absorptive-surrender itself, which being entirely out of reach of our current consciousness, graces itself to its majestic Self-Realization.

It is this ultimate surrender that is outside of all human intentions, meditations or doings. It is an act of pure Grace, and utterly inexplicable. You, as God, pick yourself up to be One with yourself.

Here's another way of explaining the same thing:

In this example, we have the planet Ego orbiting the star Consciousness. Although this example has its limitations because the ego is not separated from consciousness, it demonstrates how the process of surrendering goes.

Due to planet Ego's gravity, you live inside that planet. However, life on the star Consciousness is much better than on planet Ego. You want to go there, but how do you do it?

You eject out of planet Ego by recognizing the sense of being, or by becoming aware of the background of awareness.

Yet you still orbit around it. The chopped line represents the trajectory as you eject out of planet Ego; the straight-line circle is your line of orbit around the planet Ego. This is the first level.

As you surrender more and more, your orbit starts to expand; you go further and further away from planet Ego. The straight-line circle below represents the original orbit; the chopped circular lines are the steadily growing expansion of your orbit around planet Ego. This is the second level.

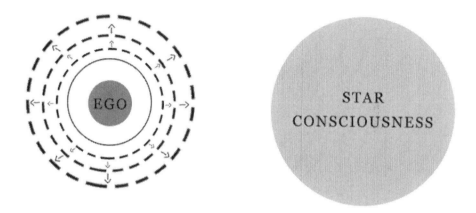

Due to the growing expansion of your orbit, you are eventually captured by the star Consciousness' stronger gravitational field. Now you are effortlessly orbiting the star Consciousness. This is the third level, the beginning of effortless being.

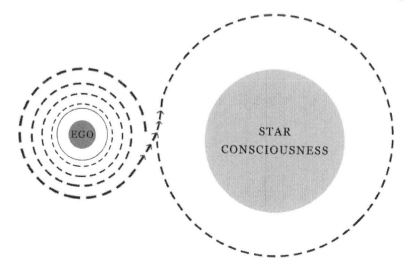

Due to your increased surrender and effortless Self-abiding, as well as to the growing pull of the star Consciousness, your orbit has shrunk, becoming smaller and smaller until you land on the star Consciousness. This is the fourth level.

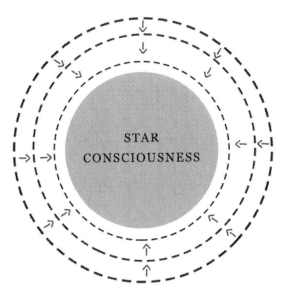

On the final level, you are absorbed by the star Consciousness as if it were a black hole that pulled you in. There's neither going out anymore nor remaining on the surface. That's true non-duality, the final level of surrender.

CHAPTER 9

LIVING FROM SAMADHI

During spiritual practice and meditation, seekers can become too complacent with the current state they are experiencing at that moment. They may erroneously consider it to be some form of advanced Samadhi, awakening or even enlightenment. Therefore, it is crucial to expound upon the disadvantages of all the Samadhis.

In *The Secret Power of Kriya Yoga*, I wrote at length about Samadhis. We can easily realize that *Savikalpa Samadhi*[15] is object-based; hence it has various fluctuations in consciousness, being impermanent and thus still prone to suffering.

Kevala Nirvikalpa Samadhi[16] suffers from the same problem: it is impermanent. Additionally, the body is lying like a corpse

---

[15] Also known as absorption with form, *Samprajnata Samadhi* or differentiated Samadhi.

[16] Also known as formless absorption, *Asamprajnata Samadhi* or undifferentiated Samadhi.

and eventually, as in deep dreamless sleep, you ("I-ego") will come out of it because your *samskaras*, *vasanas*, subtle tendencies and desires have yet to be erased.

Sahaja Nirvikalpa Samadhi[17] is the perfect "state," but there is still some clarification that needs to be made in this regard.

Let's take the example of a drop of water that lives in an infinite ocean of Consciousness:

We, as individual ego-minds, are like that drop of water in the ocean of Consciousness.

Savikalpa Samadhi is as if we were concentrating so hard on the sand on the ocean floor that we temporarily become one with it. Or we could become one with something subtler like an ocean current, or even more subtle like the oxygen inside each drop of water. These would still be object-based Samadhis, but they could enlighten us with some deep wisdom about the mechanics of the universe and creation. However, since they are "external unions," they can never reveal our true Self to us. Although interesting and capable of providing tremendous insights, they are useless for enlightenment.

---

[17] Also known as Natural Samadhi, natural state, natural formless absorption, and the true Self-Realization "state." Turiya only starts infusing our life in this permanent Samadhi.

Kevala Nirvikalpa Samadhi is as if we could temporarily dissolve our awareness of being an individual drop of water, and instead become aware that we are the whole ocean of Consciousness!

During such an experience, our "drop-of-water body" would stay motionless, laying on the ocean floor as if it had been frozen in time. In some cases, its heart might even temporarily have stopped, and only the pranic energy would sustain it. Eventually, we would revert to being an individual drop of water again, and we would still suffer from the separateness we feel. Even though we had acquired the knowledge of truly being the ocean of Consciousness rather than this individual drop, the lack of permanent restfulness in our true "identity" as the ocean would bring suffering.

Sahaja Nirvikalpa Samadhi would be as if Kevala Nirvikalpa Samadhi happened, but we never came out of it—it was permanent. We are the ocean of Consciousness. Period.

What follows next has never been clearly explained before, anywhere, to the best of my knowledge.

What happens to the drop of water in Sahaja Nirvikalpa Samadhi?

The drop of water doesn't go anywhere! It doesn't disappear or vanish into thin air in a rainbow of light. I have said in the previous volumes of the *Real Yoga* series that it keeps egolessly living its life in bliss and peace. It is a continuous state of Being as it is, and Life lives through it as an impersonal "Transcendental-I-ness." This is quite true, however, what or who is "Life"? Is "Life" different from Absolute Consciousness?

It isn't. Life is the same as Absolute Consciousness (the Unmanifested), but in its apparent relative form (the manifested). It's just a question of perspective! From the real and truthful point of view, only the Absolute exists and is. Ultimately this is the only real point of view because it is perpetual. Universes are born, expand for trillions of years, and then reverse and are dissolved, withdrawing back into the singularity only to be recreated again. Therefore, the Relative has a beginning and an end.

It's just like in your daily life: you wake up in the morning (universe's creation), live your daily life, and at the end of the day you go back to the dissolution of sleep (universe's destruction). Then the next day, the same thing happens again. It's cyclical, just like the Universe itself.

But since you are here and now, living this temporary dualistic and manifested life as a speck of consciousness, this false and illusory reality is also important! From its point of view, both the Absolute and the Relative exist.

The ocean of Consciousness has always known that it is the ocean of Consciousness and that no separation ever occurs in itself (non-duality)[18]. The drop of water has previously believed itself to be a separate entity (duality) and has now realized, through spiritual practice, direct pointers and surrender, that such is not true. It has now turned its knowledge, understanding and interaction with the world upside down, for it now knows that it is not separate (non-duality through the lens of duality).

If non-duality shines too strongly through the lens of duality, the awareness which permeates your body will expand into broader territories. This is unsustainable in the long term for your body and mind because they were not designed in such a way. Hence it's not optimal in creation for human beings. If it did happen, it would *merely be an experience*, nearly incomprehensible for the human intellect to grasp and translate.

There are other beings in the universe who don't possess physical bodies, but rather abide in the realm of the subtle mind which encompasses broader and subtler ranges of consciousness and collective consciousnesses. Their systems

---

[18] Pure Consciousness has always been realized, and no movement from ignorance toward enlightenment has ever occurred it in. There are no fluctuations and changes there. It remains as it is.

may have been designed in such way that they are capable of sustaining broader degrees of expansive body-awareness, but the same is not true for human beings.

There is no way the human mind can permanently sustain the "Mind of God" (Universal Consciousness where your body-awareness is expanded to encompass the whole of creation) and still be active in the world.

The best way for Self-Realized human beings to operate in this world is with a "nonbinding," faint body-awareness, sustained by the pure mind of the "Transcendental-I." Such body-awareness is not a prison, but rather the vehicle that allows us to celebrate the love of God in His dream.

CHAPTER 10

THE DYSFUNCTION OF KEVALA NIRVIKALPA SAMADHI

First of all, you must understand right away that Turiya is not a Samadhi experience. Rather, it is a natural byproduct of enlightenment; the godly emanation of awareness's knowledge of itself that floods the manifest world of those who live in their natural state, the non-experiential Sahaja Samadhi.

Kevala Nirvikalpa Samadhi is not a common Samadhi or experience either for that matter, but merely the total cessation of the ego-mind for a period of time. It is highly prevalent in Kriya Yoga and Kundalini Yoga teachings, and it is indeed very powerful, most of the time being the number one priority in yogic teachings. It is still a *pseudo-realization* though, because although one tastes the true bliss of Being, there is one big issue: the return of the ego-mind. This consequently makes this state temporary and thus prone to suffering due to its impermanence. This is not "heaven" as some call it—it's an alluring trap.

Being totally absorbed in the ecstatic nothingness of Nirvikalpa Samadhi may hinder our ability to function correctly and naturally in the manifest world. In light of this, Samadhi must be integrated with life, with human existence, otherwise it might detach us from the manifest world to the point of leading us to dysfunction in many facets of our human life.

This is hard to execute because the pull from the absence of ego during those Samadhis is too strong. However, if you keep entering into those states of nothingness and coming back out into the world, you are reinforcing duality at a subtle subconscious level, creating the distinction of two Selves—the illusory ego-self in this human realm, and the no-self (True Self) of Reality.

The difference between Kevala Nirvikalpa Samadhi and the integration of Turiya level 4 (which is Sahaja Nirvikalpa Samadhi) is that in Kevala Nirvikalpa Samadhi, although one is absorbed in the bliss of the Self, one doesn't truly permanently recognize oneself to be the Self, because afterward the ego-mind returns. It is akin to deep sleep in which the ego is in seed form, and it will sooner or later sprout yet again. It's like going on the most fabulous vacation *ever* for two weeks, and afterward you come back to the "real world" where you have to go to work, adhere to a rigid schedule, pay your taxes, etc. You can surmise how this might feel. Either you'd come back refreshed, happy and ready to tackle the mundane world (with the post-vacation blues slowing attempting to creep in), or you'd become lethargic, unmotivated, and even slightly depressed. You can't stop thinking about going on vacations yet again!

In Turiya level 4, if the "subtle cord" to the manifested world is not cut, one's relative consciousness can return but it will be in perfect unison and unity with the relative world, as only the Self exists in such a view (level 3, "Transcendental-I"). "Everything" is perceived as one single Being, one single Reality, one single Consciousness. There's no "I-ego," and hence no post-vacation blues because you're always on "vacation" no matter what you do or don't do. It's a huge difference.

Kevala Nirvikalpa Samadhi is thus just a taste of the bliss of pure Consciousness, a shallow realization. Such realization is no realization at all, but at best is a glimpse of what it could be.

No mind could ever conceptualize or understand the pure primordial Consciousness. As a matter of fact, not even those who achieve Self-Realization can comprehend pure Consciousness through the mind. It is just not possible.

They comprehend it without comprehending it (an understanding beyond the mind and the intellect, not from the mental realm). However, as Turiya settles into their dual vehicle, the mind starts to grasp[19]—at its most transparent possible level of comprehension in the relative realm—the Absolute.

The intellect progressively aligns itself with the "perfume" of the Absolute, as it mirrors that beautiful scent so that it becomes the most translucent possible, adding new depth to the realized human being. This perfume encircles both our life and that of those who interact with us, making it the raw experience of eternity that inexplicably attracts many beings toward us, toward our words, our presence, and our love, which come from One but embrace All. One is living from the kernel of creation—Consciousness itself. And it is everyone's natural home.

---

[19] Such understanding, regardless of how transparent and pure it is, is always incomplete and doesn't do justice to what the Unfathomable really IS.

CHAPTER 11

RESISTING THE SILENCE

Humans have gone through a lot since their inception, and have suffered for countless eons. Ignorance is the cause for our suffering, and it is a shadow hovering in the sky of our lives that the sun of our hearts can't seem to dissipate. This way of living consists mainly of stress, tension, worry, nervousness, and restlessness, and it simply cannot be allowed to continue.

The majority of people would love to relax, but can they relax?

Many of the foundations of spiritual practice are based on being able to relax—not just physically, but mentally as well. The problem is that both types of relaxation cannot be forced, in the same way that you can't force the blossoming of a rose.

Humans are too busy and obsessed with being active. They despise being still. When they are "waiting" for something, they are always showing signs of restlessness, such as tapping their foot on the ground or moving their legs. There's always a cloud of impatience or agitation around them. No wonder they get sick—illness seems to be the only way to make them slow down or stop.

You have to comprehend why you are always so active, impatient and busy.

There is a difference between spontaneous action and ego-based action. The former comes from being in unison with creation, from an empty mind, and from a consciousness consciously abiding in the present moment. The latter comes entirely from the ego-mind, its mental schemes, and from being in a permanent state of restlessness that carries with it the weight of the past and the uncertainty about the future.

The ego-mind seems to be unable to remain in its source of peace—empty awareness—and it cannot, for the sake of its life, stay still or inactive. Therefore, it has to release its restless energy through activity.

When people sit down to eat, it's almost impossible to merely eat without doing something else at the same time. They have to watch TV, read the nutritional values on the cereal box, etc. If they aren't distracting themselves in some way or another, they feel that they will explode. Even when there are moments when they could relax, they cannot unwind and let go of their "heaviness" due to old habits and tendencies. They often get bored, pick up their smartphone and browse social networks, useless websites, etc.

What if a person were to take some time to merely be aware of what's going on? That person might start to notice the futility of what they were doing, and how unconscious and unmindful that activity really was. Useless activities, needless actions, and being stressed can all literally suck the life out of you, even if you don't notice it. They also reinforce the ego-mind, and in this way strengthen ignorance. Time is the most limited resource on Earth—how do you want to spend yours?

Can you sit still for quite some time, or are you afraid of silence? And who is afraid of silence, you or your ego?

There is the stigma that you will become crazy if you remain quiet and in silence for a long time; that you will start talking to yourself and "hear voices." You might also be afraid of boredom and scared that a powerful emptiness will possess or overtake you.

People who attempt to remain quiet and silent for many days, weeks or months at a stretch usually talk about how empty they feel inside, and how a vacuum of nothingness seems to have taken hold of their life. They feel lonely. However, I'm not talking about that. Our silence is not that kind of silence; our emptiness is not that kind of emptiness. We wouldn't merely be silent for its own sake—we would be employing our silence as a spiritual practice, with lucidity and awareness, and with presence and intention. This is entirely different.

A sense of being empty will still come; a feeling of nothingness will still come; boredom will still come; internal dialogue will still come; but all of these will also pass. And if you are persistent enough to overcome this ego-mind cleanse, you will meet peace; you will meet love; you will meet joy; you will meet happiness; you will meet ecstasy; you will meet bliss; you will meet eternity; you will meet yourself; you will meet God.

Real Silence (*mouna*) will purge you. Not actually you—but rather your ego. That's why your mind is afraid of it, and that's why your mind escapes it at all costs and takes refuge in activity, in restlessness. The ego-mind just can't allow itself to melt in serenity, in non-doing, in true relaxation.

True relaxation doesn't mean that you have to posture yourself in some particular way, or that you have to lay down in a bed or on a cozy couch. True relaxation can occur during activities as well. A cyclone can be in full activity, moving at dazzling speeds and destroying everything in its path, while its eye is calm, relaxed, and tranquil.

Above all else, true relaxation is a mental state. It is the absence of mental noise and chaos, the absence of desires—an acceptance of the now. It occurs when there is no inner urge to do something, when this moment is enough and the present is good as it is. In this state, there is no impetus to do something to compensate for the usual lack of completeness because we feel complete. This means that even while you are performing an activity, you are in the now, wholly present, neither wanting to finish the activity as soon as possible, nor wanting to prolong it. This acceptance is not coming from a sense of hopelessness, but rather from the deep fulfillment that arises with inner silence.

Inner silence is not achieved through force, but through dedication, surrender, practice, and attunement to the Truth. When you are flooded with inner silence, your life becomes the most majestic symphony of the cosmos.

CHAPTER 12

"YOU ARE ALREADY ENLIGHTENED!" ... OR ARE YOU?

"There's nothing to do."

"There's nothing to accomplish. You are already fully accomplished!"

"You already are the Self!"

"You are already Pure Consciousness."

"No goal, no awakening, no practice, and no technique."

"None of that has any value and you are already enlightened! This is the direct path!"

What's all this rhetoric about? Many of today's teachers approach spirituality through this lens, which can cause immense harm to sincere seekers.

Of course you are already the Self! Of course there is nothing to accomplish from the perspective of the Absolute. Of course there is no goal because who you truly are is already enlightened.

But do you feel that way? Are you entirely free from suffering, ever at peace, bliss and with genuine (nonintellectual) wisdom?

If you follow this type of *Neo-Advaita* teaching, from either the "nothing to do" or the "you are already enlightened" school, you will go nowhere. At best, you will stagnate in a tiny "peace-empty" feeling after doing 5 minutes of intellectual Self-inquiry, and then you'll believe that you are enlightened, especially if the teacher or guru says "Yes, that is the Self! You have awakened!" Then you can become a guru too.

In all seriousness, the aforementioned is what's trending nowadays. It may have its purpose in certain circumstances, but it is mostly deceiving and unhelpful. All genuine and truthful Gurus, such as the Buddha, Lahiri Mahasaya, and Ramana Maharshi preached the importance of spiritual practice.

If today's Kriya and Kundalini Yoga are too heavy on the techniques and overlook the simple but essential state of just Being, today's non-dual teachings are mostly philosophical, intellectual and unpractical.

Those who put a lot of time into reading Advaita Vedanta

scriptures and books and never go through any spiritual practice are not going anywhere! It's like knowing all of the theory concerning space-flight without ever having been an astronaut. Practicing even 10 minutes per day will *definitely* make a big difference.

Our ignorance must be dealt with, and that—in addition to reading words and hearing talks that directly point to the Truth—requires sadhana.

These ideas that one is already enlightened and so on encourage seekers not to practice or meditate. This is terribly wrong. Spiritual practice is of utmost importance; without it, you will *not* realize your true nature. This doesn't mean that you have to practice for 30 years or 100 lifetimes; it can be as quick as one minute (as happened with Ramana Maharshi), or it can take multiple years or more (like the Buddha, who practiced for many years prior to sitting motionless for seven weeks under the Bodhi Tree and finally realizing the Truth). You must also remember that awakening Discernment[20] is of utmost importance, and this has been mentioned in great detail in the previous books of this series.

---

[20] All kinds of discernment, starting with discernment between the subject (you, the experiencer, awareness) and objects (the contents of the mind, movements of awareness), followed by the discernment between real pure teachings and fake dogmatic teachings, and so on and so forth.

When I mention spiritual practice, this implies that in addition to a "conventional sitting practice," one is also reading or hearing the words that directly expose the Truth without dogma, such as this book. Such direct pointers are crucial. If the seeker is advanced enough, spiritual practice also means being aware of your own presence/awareness throughout the day. All of this directly contributes to awakening.

If a seeker who still lives under the ignorance of separation does no spiritual practice, that person will remain ignorant. It's that simple! Most seekers aren't even capable of being aware of their own breath for more than one minute before diverting into unstable, mentally compulsive content; and if they can't do that, then there's no way that they'd be able to sustain an awareness of Being (I Am) deeply enough to melt the ego illusion.

All too often I see seekers who believe that they are as enlightened as Jesus Christ, Gautama Buddha, Bhagavan Krishna, Lao Tzu, Ramana Maharshi, Ramakrishna Paramahamsa, Lahiri Mahasaya, Milarepa, Adi Shankara, etc., just because they suddenly felt some peace or joy inside, or because they've awakened to the fact that they are not some mental content (e.g., personality) that they once thought themselves to be. Sometimes, even their gurus encourage them in this self-delusion. It's insanity. Those who've had some sort of awakening or realization should be quiet and marinate in their own beingness, and allow it to unfold before heading out to start preaching or giving satsangs.

It is easy to differentiate between those who have put in the time and love to learn, surrender and practice, and those who haven't and are no more than spiritually underdeveloped intellectuals or keyboard seekers. Don't be the latter.

Pure Consciousness is beyond the mind; hence it is beyond space-time. It is ever "realized," since it is out of time and movement. Yes, you are That, but you don't truly *know* it. "I am That" is just a thought occurring in your mind, and unless you *really know* that Truth and *permanently embody* it, it will only be a thought.

It's not enough to believe that "You are God" when you hear or read it. You must really know it through your own direct experience. Religion has believers, but you are not a believer—you are a luminous explorer of consciousness, existence, and God. The primary origin of the word *belief* is *leubh*, which comes from the Proto-Indo-European root meaning "to care, desire, love."[21] To care about God, to desire God and to love God—if that's the true original meaning of the word *belief,* then and only then are you a believer.

---

[21] From the Online Etymology Dictionary.

Now, this whole subject must not be confused with mature or ripe seekers who, in the mere presence of a genuine Master, or by hearing/reading profoundly stated truths get deep experiences, deep Samadhis or even become enlightened. Cases like this are rare, but they do happen. Most commonly those seekers have practiced and surrendered intensely (even if in previous lifetimes) and are mature enough to be at the stage where only a little blow will tumble their subtle egoic house of cards.

We must also understand that often, profoundly stated Truths can capture the mind's attention so deeply that they can alter your state of consciousness to a much deeper state of Self-Awareness (which then turns into an effortless spiritual practice), or they can even totally or partially sink the mind into Spiritual Heart.

We all know that we live in the era of the magic pill, but the real magic is *dedication, perseverance, and surrender.* Burn those "Instant Enlightenment Now!" posters and embrace your own consciousness by spending time learning about it, getting to know it, and loving it. That's the only way you'll pierce the mystery of existence.

CHAPTER 13

IS ENLIGHTENMENT HAVING NO THOUGHTS?

Some people seem to think that enlightened beings have no thoughts. They propose that to be fully enlightened, you cannot have thoughts, and this is seen as the goal.

Ancient scriptures often corroborate this notion, but what people tend to forget is that these scriptures are often either poorly translated, or are interpreted by scholars who have no direct experience through spiritual practice. Additionally, there are many words in these scriptures (e.g., Sanskrit) that have no direct translation in English. So the translators often opt for terms that fit their understanding of what the stanza in question means or of the overall teaching expounded on in that particular scripture.

We also have another issue: what is the definition of "thoughts"? Let's explore the possible interpretations and see whether they apply or not.

(a)

Are the words you are reading right now in this book considered thoughts? Is a tree in a park just a thought? Is a computer just a thought? Is the Universe just a thought? Some hardcore Advaita teachings say so. Yes, they are ultimately true, because everything you (as consciousness) perceive is through the mind. That is the perspective of Absolute Consciousness.

Since everything that can be perceived, from subtle to gross, is based on the mind, and the mind itself is based on the thought "I," the ego, then everything—except pure Consciousness—is a thought, even you.

However, when seekers ascribe to enlightenment as "having no thoughts whatsoever" they are clearly not talking about these kinds of thoughts. If they were, they wouldn't talk, because "talking" itself is a thought. Hence, just by talking, it would be self-defeating.

What are they referring to then? Are they talking about all kind of thoughts except these?

(b)

If enlightenment meant that you could not use your mind to think, to do mathematics, to visualize, to imagine, to creatively output a fantastic product, service or piece of art, to compare nutritive values on the food you eat, to write, to speak[22], and so on, then enlightenment would drastically impair your capability to act and live in the world. You probably wouldn't be able to perform your job, write and send an email, drive a car, read a book (you are probably reading with a subtle inner voice—is that a thought?), etc. You couldn't even use your power of discrimination, or store and access memories. Obviously, this is not the case for those who are genuinely enlightened. Furthermore, from all recorded accounts we have of enlightened beings, it is clear that they do have access to memories; they are not in a state of amnesia (that too, would be limiting).

As a different illustration, let's ponder on what "red" is. Well, "red" is just a thought. It is a visual and auditory symbol that designates the concept of the color that we ascribe "red" to. If enlightenment signified that those concepts—which are useful so that we can live and act in this manifested universe—would disappear, then would enlightenment be truly valuable, or would we just be in a blissful state of mindlessness?

There are more gray-areas:

Is intuition that manifests as thoughts considered a "thought"? Before everything is translated into the five

---

[22] Before speaking, a preceding thought and subsequent intention occur in the mind, even if one doesn't notice them.

gross senses, it first goes through the mind. A spontaneous insight, if it were to be expressed beyond the recesses of your heart, would have to go through a pure and transparent intellect.

Is there any problem with practical thoughts and with intuitive knowledge that manifests as pure thoughts? Not for me, and not for the ancient Masters. When I published the second book of the *Real Yoga Series*, *The Secret Power of Kriya Yoga*, it spontaneously occurred to me that this series would have five books. I simply knew that it would have five books, but I didn't know what the next three books would be about, nor when would they be written. But eventually they were. Was this a thought? It was a genuine insight. These insights do not come from the ego. They don't have to fade away once a being becomes enlightened. Such disruptive ideas actually come from the ego! Don't fall prey to those dogmas, and discover what I'm writing about through your own direct experience.

If not having all these "thoughts" were a facet of being a Self-Realized being, then realization wouldn't be the singular "thing" that everyone on the planet wants (knowingly or unknowingly), because it would bring limitations. That would make no sense whatsoever, especially since enlightenment is the end of all limitations. It is pure limitlessness.

These "thoughts" are just a needed and transient but natural part of intelligent life in this world.

So, if being fully enlightened meant that you could not have thoughts, then this definition of thoughts doesn't apply either.

(c)

What if we consider "thoughts" to be that silent voice in the head? The "narrator" that compulsively talks, talks, and talks, has selfish intentions, continuously lives in the past afraid of the present and anxious of the future, provokes restlessness, boredom, unfulfillment, sorrow, unhappiness, sadness, hatred, rejects the world, rejects what happens, doesn't dance with life, is never at joy, never at peace, can't fathom love, makes you identify with and believe in it, creating a separate identity from the rest of the world, and bringing immense suffering?

If that's your definition of thoughts—then yes—an enlightenment being has no thoughts!

If you live in the illusion perpetuated by ignorant gurus or wrongly understood/poorly translated scriptures/teachings that you cannot have anything that could be classified as a thought to be enlightened, then you will never become enlightened. Such dogmatic beliefs will keep you stuck.

Yet if we are talking about level 4 of Turiya, as mentioned

in chapter 3, then yes, none of these possible dimensions of thought mentioned earlier—*(a)*, *(b)*, and *(c)*—exist. Not a single one of them. That's the perspective of pure Consciousness, the Absolute. The body of such an enlightened being can't, however, permanently function in such a way.

From the external observer and dualistic perspective, if the body of an enlightened being is active, then that being has both *(a)* and *(b)* kind of "thoughts" through the "Transcendental-I." In none of the different levels of Turiya integration are there the kinds of thoughts that were mentioned in *(c)*, although in level 1 of Turiya, some exterior signs of subtle residual tendencies may still *seem* to occur to a very light degree in the beginning, but without any identification with them whatsoever. They are just like the smoke of an already extinguished fire.

Up until level 3, the realized being is capable of using thought as an instrument, rather than being a slave to the thinking mind as typically happens with non-realized beings, although not everyone is at the same level of maturity and Turiya absorption.

In level 4 of Turiya, nobody would be reading this book. Only unfathomable and unexplainable non-perceptive bliss beyond bliss IS.

CHAPTER 14
THE MYTH OF PSYCHOLOGICAL PERFECTION

People who cannot cope with this world usually seek refuge in spirituality. This by itself is not a bad thing, but hiding from and ignoring one's deep inner problems is. Those issues will prevent anyone from reaching legitimate spiritual depth because they will function as anchors when what spiritual aspirants are trying to do is fly.

Wanting to escape and find an easy solution is not the way. Deep understanding, reflection, and meditation are needed. Lucidity and awareness are needed, not obfuscation and ignorance.

People want to escape life, troubles and problems by diving into spirituality, and think that "enlightenment" will solve all of their issues and concerns.

But that is not true. Why?

Well, to start, yes, you will not see anything as troubles or problems after realizing your true nature. But the catch here is that you must first become extremely aware of what's going on within yourself, and solve those issues so that you can have enough peace and emptiness of mind to dive deeply into self-discovery.

Ultimately, subconsciously buried traumas have to come to the surface so that you can purify them, thereby reprogramming the way you feel about those emotional conditionings. This then enables you to dive deeply enough to cut off the root of all of them—the "I-ego"—so that they don't emerge or accumulate anymore. Spiritual practice and purification are synonymous with diving beneath the conscious mind.

This is not contrary to what is said in *The Yoga of Consciousness*:

> "All conditionings, which pertain to the psychological mind[23] are based on the notion of "I," or "I am the body." They are like tomato sauce's stains in one's clothing. We can wash and remove those stains, but it's not easy, and there's no guarantee we won't get our clothes dirty again. Wasting lifetimes progressively

---

[23] The part of the mind that creates your story and interprets it, identifying with thought and its projections, inevitably causing suffering.

removing these conditionings will not cut it, especially since new ones might appear."

(...)

"Deep-rooted habits stemming from countless lifetimes, unconscious desires, fears, traumas, etc., all work against you. Yet, being persistent with your spiritual practice will unlock all of the unconscious debris, so that they come to the surface to be purified and realized as not self. However, as many things have yet to be manifested in your current life, still being in seed form, there will be times where you will be able to clear them without them being materialized or at least, without materializing too strongly."

"However, some degree of mind purification is needed at the beginning, because a less conditioned mind not only brings more peace and joy to our life, but is the basis that allows us to truly shed some blazing light on the phantom ego, unveiling its non-existent nature[24]. Nevertheless, it's worth emphasizing that continuously cleaning the dust off the screen (of consciousness) will be a lifetime(s) duty. That's what the ego wants!"

---

[24] Reading this book also purifies your mind. Whenever you come in contact with genuine words and energy, if you allow them to go deep within your being, your mind will shed a lot of conditionings, from beliefs to blockages, and allow a higher wisdom and awareness to arise.

The strongest inner issues and problems have to be purified first, or else you will not go far. But then, consciously fixing and cleaning up everything will not lead you anywhere.

All of this makes people idealize psychological perfection. They project it onto their teacher/guru/master and believe that spirituality will make them psychologically perfect and self-actualized as well.

It is the nature of the manifest world to evolve. If, for example, humankind were to stop evolving, it would become stale and eventually die. This evolution always occurs within space-time.

Thus, one could say that being enlightened is the next step in evolution. However, this is where the mix-up of enlightenment with the belief in the evolution toward a perfect personality occurs. Enlightenment is outside of space-time—it's not a movement of the ego-mind, but rather its cessation.

Thinking that enlightenment will make the personality of someone perfect is a grandiose idea created by the ego, and reinforced by lots of spiritual and mystical books that depict enlightened beings as saints incapable of doing anything outside of the standard ethical paradigm. This has led many to believe in the myth of psychological perfection.

Gurus aren't perfect. Enlightened beings aren't perfect.

That's because "perfect" is just a concept that is subjective to your preconceived notions of what a perfect human being is. The enlightened being doesn't necessarily have to correspond to that. Basically, that's just what you think, and it doesn't mean it's true or factual because everyone has their own opinion and beliefs regarding how an enlightened being should act, behave, talk, walk, etc.

For some people, an enlightened Master has to be extremely serious and cannot laugh or tell a joke. For others, an enlightened Master needs to live in total poverty inside of a cave, without knowing how to use a computer or a smartphone.

Those who hold such dogmatic beliefs are the ones still living in the Stone Age and think that someone who is awake must have a long white beard, wear white clothes and live in the Himalayas. This is absolutely false and ridiculous.

You should not project your ideas of what an enlightened being is because you will be disappointed. There are no perfect enlightened gurus. That's just a fantasy created by the ego-mind. What is perfect for some might be horrible for others.

The mental or physical attributes that an enlightened being should have in one person's opinion are the same attributes that others might consider as "definitely not enlightened."

An enlightened being might yell at you—just to help you see a point or to understand something more deeply. Another enlightened being might merely sit in silence without uttering a word—just to help you see a point or to understand something more deeply. One is not better than the other; they are just different expressions of the same Truth. The perfume of the Absolute has to be expressed in different ways to suit the different tendencies, temperaments, and maturities of seekers.

There is also the misleading idea that an enlightened being has no preferences, likes or dislikes, but that's not how it really is.

An enlightened being is truly the Absolute. Throughout the path, dispassion and non-attachment arise in seekers, and once they "become" Self-realized, there is no longer any identification with anything at all. This doesn't mean, however, that the "Transcendental-I" that remains, and which has a pure mind as its support, doesn't have any likes or dislikes that were already embedded in the relative consciousness.

If you enjoyed eating apple pie before you realized your true nature, you will still enjoy eating apple pie afterward. If you disliked the smell of tobacco smoke before, you will still dislike it after realization. Nonetheless, this doesn't mean you will be identified with the one who likes apple pies or dislikes tobacco smoke—no. Your true "identity" is pure Consciousness, which has no likes or dislikes, and that's truly your direct experience. What is meant is only relative to the dual experience in this world from an outsider's point of view or through the mind's perspective.

Being Self-realized, if you were to see a person suffering and dying in front of you, sobbing his heart out, you would not show inhumane coldness or heartlessness. It's true that your peace would not be affected, but you might even cry and naturally show emotion. There's no problem with that.

Enlightenment doesn't turn you into a cold, robotic, insensitive, and disengaged bastard. Enlightened beings are kind, selfless, and compassionate. Even a Zen Buddhist Master hitting his disciple with a flat wooden stick can do it out of compassion (even if one doesn't agree with such "training" methods).

This should not be taken out of context and used as an example to excuse a guru who has emotionally exploited students (or worse). No. Real Gurus don't do that.

Its purpose is to show you that enlightenment will not bring about psychological perfection because that's always relative to the ego's preconceived ideas. What enlightenment does bring is psychological freedom—freedom from wanting to "become" a certain way, or to be in a certain manner. It's the freedom that an innocent child has.

If your body-mind is prone to subtle habits and tendencies, and they do not substantially harm the process of awakening and discovering your true nature, they will not necessarily disappear with enlightenment. They can, but they might not. These would not be called "negative conditioning," but rather "constructed habits that do not harm the awakening process to a significant degree."

An example is the kind of food you eat. Not eating meat or fish, for example, will aid your process because they are heavy to digest, requiring a lot of energy/prana, and hence they reduce the available amount of energy that you can use for spiritual practice (notice how sleepy you get after you eat a big meal; your body has to expend a lot of energy to digest that food).

Additionally, meat and heavy foods don't have a "positive vibration" so to speak. Energetically speaking, meat often carries negative energy from both the individual suffering of the slaughtered animal, as well as from the collective mind of those very same animals (livestock), which most times are not treated with respect and kindness, as you know. This is not related to morality, but to simple facts that anyone can easily realize if they put a little time into contemplating the type of food they eat.

With that being said, the type of food that one eats is not a deal-breaker. There have been realized Masters who ate meat or fish. This "habit" does not have to disappear with enlightenment.

Culture, life's background, and subtle tendencies always play a role in the dualistic expression of the enlightened being. However, some aspects of the perfume of realization are universally consistent, such as unbroken peace in the midst of all situations, a permanent joy in spite of whatever may look like to an outsider, no-fear of death and unlimited wisdom. Above all, realized beings always carry the flavor of transcendental presence with them.

On the spiritual path, the search for psychological completion is futile. Psychological security and comfort are all in the mind. This is merely the "I-ego" looking for refuge because it still lacks something. It lacks completeness—it lacks the recognition of its true Self.

This is not to say that psychological growth and maturation won't happen as you spiritually evolve. They definitely will as a consequence of both the path (e.g., compassion will grow), and of the infusion of Turiya into the manifest world.

But improving and expanding the personality is a journey in the ego's game.

Self-Realization is the only "field" where, despite being totally satisfied and fulfilled with whatever occurs, our dualistic expression in life continues to grow and expand in terms of becoming a better expression of the Absolute. This doesn't require effort and movement in psychological time like psychological growth does—it's naturally effortless.

Enlightenment is not the pursuit of some ideal identity with specific characteristics that you ascribe to being "divine," "sacred," and so on. Enlightenment is beyond the illusion of psychological growth or perfection—it is the ceasing of all ideals, beliefs, notions, and illusions.

> "I do not regard as a 'gain' which is soon lost; only that is a gain which is not lost – and there is no such gain available to man in this world, however hard he may struggle. On the other hand, both fleeting gains and temporary adversities come to a man even without his seeking. (...) Whichever be the path you choose, stop not till the psychological conditioning ceases entirely."
>
> - YOGA VASISTHA

PART III
DOWN THE RABBIT HOLE

Meditation on this sentence is enough for Self-Realization:

That which is seeking is the Truth.

CHAPTER 15
THE PHANTOM ENIGMA

Legend has it that there was once a ghost town somewhere in Southern Asia that was haunted by a powerful phantom genie capable of materializing all things and fulfilling all desires. The legend also said that unless one possessed the mighty mantra capable of controlling the phantom genie, he would transform anyone who asked him to fulfill desires into a donkey. The haunted town was thus filled entirely with donkeys—there were no people because all had either left or been transformed into donkeys.

In a neighboring town, there was an extremely lazy and poor man named Bubba. His only means of survival was by stealing fruit and other items from the local merchants.

One time, while he was stealing a mango from a merchant, he got caught in the act.

"If I see you stealing again, I will grab you by the ear and drag you to the phantom genie in the other town. He will transform you into a donkey, and you will not disturb anyone ever again!" the angry merchant said.

"What are you talking about? What phantom genie?" Bubba yelled, "Those are just myths! I don't believe in any of that."

"Well, if you haven't heard...," the merchantman said with a smirk on his face and a treacherous look, "... legend says he can fulfill all desires."

"What? All desires?" asked Bubba, who was suddenly very interested.

"Yes, all desires. Everything you want will be yours," enticingly said the merchant, accentuating the tone of his voice with the intention of persuading Bubba.

"Really? I will go there then, so that I can fulfill all of my desires! I will then be the richest man in the world, with lustrous palaces, bright diamonds, wine, and beautiful women!" Bubba loudly exclaimed, barely able to contain his excitement.

Bubba was ready to go, and had already pictured it all in his imagination. He would go to the neighboring town, capture and force the phantom genie to fulfill all of his desires!

"If I were you, I would be cautious," warned an unknown

man, abruptly breaking Bubba's enthusiasm, "Unless you have the secret mantra to be able to control the phantom, you have no chance."

Bubba looked into the man's eyes and saw that he was telling the truth. "Well, where can I find that secret mantra?" Bubba asked.

"You'll have to go ask the Mahasadhu, the great Master," replied the unknown man. "He might give you the sacred mantra."

Bubba instantly started running toward the house of the Mahasadhu, who was a great Sage, was highly respected throughout the region, and possessed unrivaled wisdom and peace.

He found the Mahasadhu sitting cross-legged on the street, right in front of his house.

"Sir, I need your help!" Bubba pleaded, "I need you to give me the secret mantra so that I can control the phantom genie of the other town."

The Mahasadhu looked at Bubba with tenderness, and questioned: "Why would you want to control the phantom genie? Did he do any harm to you?"

"I heard that he can fulfill all my desires. As you know sir,

I am poor, and really need the money." Bubba whimpered. "Please, sir."

The Mahasadhu looked Bubba in the eye, sighed, and went inside his home.

Bubba was heartbroken. He knocked on the door of the Master's house and waited for the Master to answer.

After a few minutes, the Master opened the door, walked outside, and looked at Bubba. "So you want to control the phantom genie so that he can give you money?"

"Yes." cried Bubba.

"If you want money, then you have to work. Why don't you work?" the Mahasadhu questioned.

"I need to feel stronger to be able to work. I just want the money to get food, sir." Bubba was starting to get very uneasy. "It's just to buy food, only food, good sir."

"Ok. Just for food," the Master stated. "I will give you a magical mantra that you can use only to acquire food. But beware, if you ask for anything else besides food, you will have to ask the phantom genie to continuously fulfill your desires."

This statement made Bubba curious. "Why is that?" he asked.

The Master explained, "The genie used to be a person just like you, but he was overtaken by lust for wealth and power. The phantom genie gathers energy either by continuously fulfilling different desires outside the power of the magical mantra, or by fulfilling his own desires."

"What are his desires?" Bubba questioned.

"He wants to transform everyone who asks him to fulfill desires into a donkey," the Master said. "He doesn't like people who bother him with their requests. This mantra works only for food, and again, if you ask for anything else, you will have to keep providing this phantom genie with desires to fulfill. If you run out of desires to fulfill, he will fulfill his own desire by transforming you into a donkey."

"Thank you, dear sir," Bubba responded, "What's the mantra?"

"As soon as you are near the phantom genie, chant Om four times in different tones. That's all," whispered the Master.

"Really? Thank you. Goodbye sir!" Bubba excitedly said. He left the vicinity of the Master's house and started running toward the town of the phantom genie. Everyone else was afraid to go to the haunted town for fear of being transformed into a donkey, but Bubba was running toward it with growing enthusiasm!

"I will have no problem continuously asking that freaking ghost for things. He will be fulfilling my desires for all of eternity. I want so many things that I shall never run out of desires to ask him for," Bubba thought while he was approaching the haunted town.

As soon as he reached the town, Bubba started yelling, calling for the phantom genie. Soon the ghost appeared in front of him and said: "What do you want?"

Bubba wasted no time and instantly chanted Om four times in different tones. Suddenly the phantom genie was surrounded by a magical mist and succumbed to the will of Bubba.

"Give me food." Bubba requested.

"Here's your banquet," the phantom genie said.

Bubba was delighted and rapidly began to eat the food, giving in to gluttony. Once he finished, he turned to the phantom genie and requested: "Give me money."

Suddenly one hundred chests filled with gold appeared. Bubba was ecstatic.

"Now that you have asked me to fulfill different desires, I must continuously fulfill your desires. However, if you fail to ask me, I will transform you into a donkey."

"No problem," Bubba said with full confidence. "I have

countless things to ask you for. Let's start with new clothes."

"Done." responded the phantom genie at lightning speed.

"Hmm, that was fast," shot back Bubba. "Build me a majestic castle."

"Done."

"Destroy this haunted town and in its place build a beautiful kingdom with lakes, big gates and statues in my honor." Bubba requested.

"Done."

"Bring me ten beautiful women, and make them fall in love with me."

Ten gorgeous women suddenly appeared out of nowhere. They all looked at Bubba and instantly fell in love with him.

"Done," said the phantom genie. "What else?"

"Build me an army, a mighty carriage with powerful horses, and ships."

"It is done," the phantom uttered.

The speed at which the phantom genie was fulfilling Bubba's wishes was dazzling. Bubba was getting frightened because he noticed that he was going to run out of desires faster than he expected. He couldn't find any more desires to be fulfilled. He already had everything that he wanted and more.

"If you have no more desires for me to fulfill, I will have to transform you into a donkey," the phantom shouted.

"Wait, wait!" Bubba countered, while thinking about what to do to escape this conundrum. "Take me to the Mahasadhu's home!"

Immediately, Bubba was standing next to the Mahasadhu, who was yet again sitting cross-legged on the street.

"Sir, please help me. I have failed you, for I have requested the fulfillment of multiple desires. Now I don't know what to do anymore; I can't make up desires faster than this mad ghost can fulfill them. He is on the verge of transforming me into a donkey. Please sir, help me!" Bubba yelped in panic.

"Well, you have done what I advised you not to do. Now you want me to fix this?" the Master said.

"Yes sir, I have learned my lesson. I will never again do such a thing." Bubba whimpered, as he was on the verge of being transformed into a donkey by the phantom genie. He was begging the Master to save his life.

"Ok. I will help you. Ask your phantom to fulfill one last desire. Tell him to find his own mind," the Master instructed.

"What?" Bubba was confused.

"Just do it," ordered the Master.

"My desire is for you to find your own mind," commanded Bubba to the phantom genie.

"No problem. You will not escape me," uttered the phantom genie.

But now something strange started to happen. The phantom couldn't find his own mind. He tried really hard, but he couldn't do it. This was one desire that he seemingly couldn't fulfill. The phantom genie went on for days, and he just couldn't find his mind.

"I can't fulfill this desire. I could be here for all of eternity, and I wouldn't find my own mind. It's impossible!" said the phantom, quite saddened.

Bubba was thrilled. As he was about to thank the Mahasadhu, the latter made a signal for him to shut up, and asked the phantom: "Why can't you find your own mind?"

The phantom stopped for a second and his eyes became as bright as the sun. "Because it doesn't exist!" uttered the phantom genie.

The Master smiled, and the phantom continued with a final remark: "I have no existence of my own!"

As soon as the phantom genie exclaimed this sentence, an aura of blazing golden light enveloped his ghost-like body, transforming him into a figure of light.

He then remained quiet, peaceful, desireless, and in bliss, unbrokenly immersed in the Self. All of the people who he had transformed into donkeys instantly reverted to their human forms.

The Master was pleased, and Bubba was tremendously grateful. He renounced his kingdom and his expensive clothes. He let the poor live in his newly created city, and donated all of his money to them, except for one chest filled with gold which he gave to the Master. This allowed an ashram to be built that had enough space and food to accommodate people from all over the country, who came to learn from the Master.

Soon he became the Mahasadhu's chief disciple, hoping someday to reach what a seemingly mad ghost appeared to have found: perpetual completeness!

And this is the story of the phantom who became enlightened once he realized he couldn't find his own mind!

CHAPTER 16
ONLY NOTHING SURVIVES FOREVER

Science tells us that the Universe came into being from an unknown infinite singularity that cannot be adequately understood by any scientific or physical means whatsoever, because it is not physical nor is it within time-space. It was after the "explosion" of this singularity that the Universe was created—about 13.8 billion years ago—and it has been expanding ever since.

But why did the Universe come into being, and why will it eventually revert to its original singularity, just to be recreated again and again, ad infinitum?

As a concession to the mind, we could say that the purpose of manifestation is to allow non-dual consciousness to experience itself. It is through countless different manifested forms that the unmanifested can experience and get to know itself.

Let's suppose that you were born on the French Polynesian

island of Bora Bora. Your parents worked in a resort there and you all lived in a small bungalow over the water—in one of the most paradisiacal places in the world. As you grew up, you became accustomed to this beautiful place, and to the fact that thousands of people flew there, spent a few days or weeks vacationing, and then left.

Every time you saw those tourists, you noticed that they were mesmerized—it was as if Bora Bora were heaven to them. They loved the place so much that they couldn't stop saying how divine and majestic it was.

But for you? It was just the same old Bora Bora. Yeah, it was nice, but it was ... normal.

When you were 18 years old, you left Bora Bora to go study at the University of Paris in France.

Over time, you got acclimated to Paris, and after you graduated, you stayed in France, working there while your parents were still living and working far away in Bora Bora.

20 years pass, and although your parents visit you in France every two years, you have never returned to Bora Bora. This year, however, things will be different—you will visit Bora Bora after being away for two decades.

As soon as you arrive and leave the airport grounds, you see the view outside and have a jaw-dropping moment. You